INVENTORY MANAGEMENT

PRASHANT KUMAR
Former Head and Dean
Faculty of Commerce
Banaras Hindu University
Varanasi

PHI Learning Private Limited
Delhi-110092
2025

*In fond memory of **Shri Asoke K. Ghosh** (October 1942–February 2024), Founder Chairman and Managing Director of PHI Learning, whose vision endlessly inspires.*

The Legacy Continues... .

Published by Pushpita Ghosh, PHI Learning Private Limited, Rimjhim House, 111, Patparganj Industrial Estate, Delhi-110092 and Printed by Syndicate Binders, A-20, Hosiery Complex, Noida, Phase-II Extension, Noida-201305 (N.C.R. Delhi).

₹425.00

Inventory Management
Prashant Kumar

ISBN-978-93-5443-839-4 (Print Book)
ISBN-978-93-5443-758-8 (e-Book)

To

My Parents

in their loving memory

Contents

Preface .... *xi*

PART–I

1. Working Capital–I **3**

1.1 Introduction 3
1.2 Features of Working Capital 4
1.3 Concepts of Working Capital 5
1.4 Kinds of Working Capital 7
1.5 Operating Cycle Concept of Working Capital 9
1.5.1 Importance of Operating Cycle 9
1.5.2 Types of Operating Cycle 10
1.6 Nature of Working Capital 13
1.7 Need for Working Capital 13
1.8 Objectives of Working Capital 14
1.9 Factors Influencing Working Capital Need 15
1.9.1 Nature of Business 15
1.9.2 Size of Business 16
1.9.3 Manufacturing Cycle 16
1.9.4 Production Policy 16
1.9.5 Seasonal Variations 16
1.9.6 Working Capital Cycle 17
1.9.7 Price Level Changes 17
1.9.8 Credit Policy of the Firm 17
1.9.9 Frequency of Stock Turnover 18
1.9.10 Business Cycle 18
1.9.11 Rate of Growth and Diversification of Business 18
1.9.12 Credit Availability 18
1.9.13 Operating Performance 19
1.9.14 Economic Factors 19
1.9.15 Management Attitude 19
1.10 Estimating Working Capital Needs 19
1.11 Techniques of Estimating Working Capital Need 20

Theoretical Questions *36*

2. Working Capital–II **42**

2.1 Introduction 42
2.2 Financing of Working Capital 43
2.2.1 Financing of Long-term Working Capital 43
2.2.2 Financing of Short-term Working Capital 45
2.3 Strategies for Working Capital Financing Mix 49
2.3.1 Conservative Approach 49
2.3.2 Aggressive Approach 51
2.3.3 Hedging Approach 53
2.4 Working Capital Ratio 53
2.4.1 Current Ratio 54
2.4.2 Quick Ratio 54
2.4.3 Absolute Liquid Ratio 55
2.4.4 Interval Measure 56
2.4.5 Working Capital Turnover 58
2.5 Adequacy of Working Capital 61
2.6 Dangers of Excess Working Capital 62
2.7 Symptoms of Poor Working Capital Management 63
Theoretical Questions *63*

PART–II

3. Inventory **69**

3.1 Introduction 69
3.2 Inventory 70
3.3 Types of Inventories 71
3.3.1 Raw Materials 71
3.3.2 Work-in-Progress 71
3.3.3 Finished Goods 71
3.3.4 Spares 71
3.3.5 Tools 72
3.3.6 Sundry Materials or Consumables 72
3.3.7 Packing Materials 72
3.4 Inventory Cost 72
3.4.1 Capital Cost 72
3.4.2 Ordering Cost 72
3.4.3 Storage Costs 73
3.4.4 Stockout Costs 73
3.4.5 Overstocking Costs 73
3.5 Need for Holding Inventory 73
3.5.1 Transaction Motive 74
3.5.2 Precautionary Motive 74
3.5.3 Speculative Motive 74

3.5.4 Reasons for Holding Raw Materials 74
3.5.5 Reasons for Holding Work-in-Progress 75
3.5.6 Reasons for Holding Finished Goods 75
3.6 Risk of Holding Inventories 75
3.6.1 Risk of Price Decline 75
3.6.2 Risk of Obsolescence 75
3.6.3 Risk of Deterioration in Quality 76
3.6.4 Risk of Loss of Material 76
3.7 Objectives of Inventory Management 76
3.7.1 Availability of Raw Materials 76
3.7.2 Availability of Stock of Finished Goods 76
3.7.3 Economic Purchasing 77
3.7.4 No Understocking 77
3.7.5 No Overstocking 77
3.7.6 Effective Use of Funds 77
3.7.7 Minimisation of Material Loss Risk 77
3.7.8 Furnishing of Data 78
3.8 Principles of Inventory Management 78
3.8.1 Co-ordination Among Departments 78
3.8.2 Raw Material Demand Estimation 78
3.8.3 Determination of Stock Levels 78
3.8.4 Purchasing and Replenishment of Raw Materials 79
3.8.5 Storage Management 79
3.8.6 Issue Management 79
3.8.7 Use of Standard Forms 79
3.8.8 Valuation of Inventory 79
3.8.9 Finished Goods Demand Forecasting 80
3.8.10 Warehouse Management 80
3.8.11 Supply Chain Management 80
3.8.12 Risk Management 80
3.8.13 Accounting of Inventory 80
3.8.14 Co-ordination in Departments 81
3.9 Benefits of Inventory Management 81
3.10 Role of Inventory Management 82
3.11 Material Loss Management 82
3.11.1 Waste 83
3.11.2 Scrap 84
3.11.3 Spoilage 85
3.11.4 Defectives 86
3.12 Obsolete Items 87
3.12.1 Causes of Obsolescence 88
3.12.2 Disposal of Obsolete Items 88
3.12.3 Control of Obsolescence 89
Theoretical Questions *89*

4. Inventory Valuation 91

4.1 Introduction 91
4.2 Objectives of Inventory Valuation 92
4.3 Methods of Inventory Valuation 93
4.3.1 Specific Identification Method 93
4.3.2 First-in-First Out (FIFO) Method 94
4.3.3 Last-in-First Out (LIFO) Method 96
4.3.4 Simple Average Price Method 99
4.3.5 Weighted Average Price Method 101
4.3.6 Standard Price Method 102
4.3.7 Inflated Price Method 104
4.3.8 Replacement Price Method 105
4.3.9 Realisable Price Method 105
4.4 Impact of Inventory Inaccuracy 105
4.4.1 Overstocking 105
4.4.2 Understocking 107
4.5 Strategies to Avoid Overstocking and Understocking 108
4.6 Classification of Materials 108
4.6.1 Methods of Classification 109
4.6.2 Advantages of Classification of Inventory 110
4.7 Codification of Materials 110
4.7.1 Requisites of Coding 111
4.7.2 Methods of Codification 111
4.7.3 Advantages of Coding 112
4.8 Lead Time 112
4.9 Replenishment Policy 113
4.9.1 Replenishment Methods 113
4.9.2 Method Selection 114
Theoretical Questions 114

5. Inventory Control 119

5.1 Introduction 119
5.2 Objectives of Inventory Control 120
5.2.1 Physical Objectives 120
5.2.2 Financial Objectives 121
5.3 Importance of Inventory Control 122
5.4 Essentials of Inventory Control 123
5.5 Inventory Control Techniques 123
5.5.1 Determination of Stock Levels 124
5.5.2 Economic Order Quantity 127
5.5.3 ABC Analysis 132
5.5.4 Perpetual Inventory System 136

5.5.5 Just-in-Time (JIT) System 138
5.5.6 Control Ratios 140
5.6 Selective Techniques of Inventory Control....................144
5.6.1 VED Analysis 144
5.6.2 FSN Analysis 144
5.6.3 HML Analysis....................145
5.6.4 SDE Analysis 145
5.6.5 SOS Analysis 145
5.6.6 GOLF Analysis 145
Theoretical Questions....................145

Index ***153***

Preface

It gives me immense pleasure to present before you the first edition of my textbook titled "Inventory Management". The book is the outcome of my long teaching experience which helped me in writing this text and making the book students' friendly as well as useful for professionals from other discipline of knowledge. Production and inventory management are integrated functions. The techniques of inventory control help in managing production and materials more effectively specially in manufacturing firms. Products cost, quality, matching market demand, delivery reliability, etc., largely depend upon effective inventory management. The book has been designed for the B.Com. and B.B.A. students and other professionals, based on NEP syllabus especially the syllabus of U.P. State Universities. The subject matter has been explained in simplified and elaborated manner. For the convenience of the students, the book has been divided in two parts: Part–I deals with the topics of working capital management in two chapters, whereas Part–II deals with inventory management topics spanning three chapters. The book has been reinforced with figures, illustrations and review questions in three parts—short answers, long answers and numerical problems with answers for easy understanding of the subject and preparing for the examination.

I am thankful to my wife Mrs. Neeta Srivastava, daughter Mrs. Shreya Srivastava and son Mr. Rachit Kumar for inspiring me after the superannuation to contribute for literature and share my long teaching experience for the benefits of students, in particular, and society, in general.

I am always thankful to all authors whose standard works have been referred along with definitions in writing this book.

I am also thankful to the publisher PHI Learning Private Limited, Delhi for giving me this opportunity and publishing the book in time.

I invite valuable suggestions from the readers of the book for improvement in future edition at phi@phindia.com.

Prashant Kumar

Part–I

Chapter 1: Working Capital–I
Chapter 2: Working Capital–II

1

Working Capital–I

CHAPTER OVERVIEW AND LEARNING OBJECTIVES

The short-term financing decisions relates to working capital management. There are different concepts of working capital, i.e., gross and net working capital, fixed and variable working capital, etc. The operating cycle concept of working capital is gaining more and more importance from the practical utility point of view. The nature of working capital is the liquid investment because it is realised within a year. For running the business smoothly, maintenance of adequate working capital is essential. Various factors are influencing the need of working capital. Therefore, working capital needs should be estimated accurately by using the different techniques.

Learning Objectives: *The students will be able to:*

- Define the term 'working capital' and its objectives
- Explain the concept of working capital
- Understand the need of working capital
- Discuss the factors influencing working capital need
- Estimate working capital requirement by applying the different techniques

1.1 INTRODUCTION

Every business needs funds for two purposes-one for meeting its capital expenditure requirement for establishing the business, i.e., long-term funds or fixed capital and second for meeting its day-to-day operational requirements of the business, i.e., short-term funds or current capital. For efficient financial management, a finance manager of the firm looks on the Balance Sheet of the firm for meeting long-term and short-term requirements of funds. In order to meet the capital goods requirements, e.g., land and building, plant and machinery, furniture, etc., the finance manager looks on the asset side of the balance sheet and for capital or funds on the liability side of the balance sheet. The objective of the finance manager is to balance the two sides of the balance sheet in such a way that the net worth of the firm should increase without increasing the riskiness (liability) of the firm. This balancing may be called financing. It includes the efficient management of long-term and short-term funds. The basic difference in the management of long-term and short-term funds lies in timing of cash inflow. The timing of cash inflow in long-term financing involves extended period of time, i.e., more than a year while timing of cash inflow in short-term financing involves within a year. Thus, the short-term financing decisions relates to working capital management. In other words, lower portion of two sides of the balance sheet, i.e., current assets and current liabilities comes under the purview of working capital management. Therefore, the working capital management is more difficult than fixed assets due to timing of cash inflow. Working capital maintains the smooth running of business activities. Apart from fixed investment, every business requires funds for operational aspects as well as investment in current assets, i.e., stock of raw materials, work-in-progress, stock of finished goods, book debts and cash balance. Capital invested for these purposes is known as working capital or current capital or circulating capital or fluctuating capital.

Definitions

According to **Shubin**, "Working Capital is the amount of funds necessary to cover the cost of operating the enterprise."

According to **Hoagland**, "Working capital is descriptive of that capital which is not fixed. But the more common use of the working capital is to consider as the difference between the book value of current assets and current liabilities."

According to **Genestenberg**, "Circulating capital means current assets of a company that are changed in the ordinary course of business from one form to another, as for example, from cash to inventories, inventories to receivables, receivables into cash."

In simple accounting term, working capital is defined as the excess of current assets over current liabilities or difference between cash inflow and outflow.

1.2 FEATURES OF WORKING CAPITAL

After analysing the above definitions, the following features of the working capital may be outlined:

(i) Working capital is the management of short-term funds.
(ii) Cash inflow is expected within short period, i.e., within a year.
(iii) Working capital is related to the management of current assets which are changing in the ordinary course of business from one form to another.
(iv) Working capital is not a fixed capital.
(v) Working capital management ensures smooth running of business activities.
(vi) Management of working capital assures good financial health and liquidity of the business.

1.3 CONCEPTS OF WORKING CAPITAL

There are basically two concepts of the working capital:

1. Gross Working Capital: It is the broader concept of working capital. In this sense, gross working capital is the capital invested in total current assets of the firm. In other words, it is the aggregate of total amount of current assets. Hence, gross working capital is also called total current assets approach. The concept emphasises upon the quantitative aspect of the working capital. The quantum of current assets denotes the quantum of working capital. The gross working capital focuses on the optimum investment in current assets and what sources of financing will be taken into consideration. The reason is that certain level of various components of current assets is to be maintained by the organisation to meet the demand of the production and market. The gross working capital concept may be presented with the help of the following equation:

Gross Working Capital = Total of Current Assets

Components of Current Assets

The following items are included in Current Assets:

(a) Cash and Bank Balances
(b) Debtors
(c) Receivables
(d) Stock of Raw Material
(e) Work-in-progress
(f) Stock of Finished Goods
(g) Short-term Advances
(h) Temporary Investments
(i) Stores and spares
(j) Prepaid Expenses
(k) Accrued income

2. Net Working Capital: It is the narrow concept of working capital. According to this concept, the net working capital is the difference between current assets and current liabilities. Net working capital is an accounting concept of working capital. Net working capital may be positive or negative. The excess of current assets over current liabilities indicates the presence of working capital or it may be said as positive working capital. On the contrary, if the current liabilities exceed the current assets obviously there is no working capital as per this concept. But it is working capital deficit or it may be said as negative working capital. This concept emphasises upon the qualitative aspect of working capital. The excess of current assets over current liabilities expresses the net current assets and denotes the qualitative aspect of current assets. This excess amount indicates the firm's ability to meet its operating expenses and contingencies. It is the indicator of financial soundness of the firm and protection to the creditors. The net working capital concept may be represented with the help of the following equation:

Net Working Capital = Current Assets – Current Liabilities

Components of Current Liabilities

(a) Creditors
(b) Bills Payable
(c) Outstanding Expenses
(d) Short-term Loans and Advances
(e) Overdraft
(f) Dividend Payable
(g) Tax Payable

ILLUSTRATION 1.1: The following is the Balance Sheet of Kanti Lal Pvt. Ltd. as on 31st March, 2022:

Balance Sheet of Kanti Lal Pvt. Ltd. as on 31st March, 2022

Liabilities	*Amount ₹*	*Assets*	*Amount ₹*
Share Capital	3,00,000	Land and Building	2,00,000
General Reserve	1,00,000	Plant and Machinery	75,000
Profit and Loss A/c	40,000	Furniture	75,000
Creditors	1,00,000	Stock of Finished Goods	1,00,000
Bills Payable	50,000	Work-in-progress	20,000
Outstanding Expenses	30,000	Debtors	1,50,000
Bank Overdraft	70,000	Short-term Investments	50,000
Dividends Payable	60,000	Bills Receivables	40,000
Provision for Taxation	50,000	Cash	20,000
		Bank	50,000
		Prepaid Expenses	20,000
	8,00,000		**8,00,000**

You are required to calculate:

(i) Gross Working Capital
(ii) Net Working Capital

Solution:

Current Assets	Amount ₹
Stock of Finished Goods	1,00,000
Work-in-progress	20,000
Debtors	1,50,000
Short-term Investments	50,000

Bills Receivables	40,000
Cash	20,000
Bank	50,000
Prepaid Expenses	20,000
	4,50,000
Current Liabilities	
Creditors	1,00,000
Bills Payable	50,000
Outstanding Expenses	30,000
Bank Overdraft	70,000
Dividend Payable	60,000
Provision for Taxation	50,000
	3,60,000

(i) Gross Working Capital = Total of Current Assets
= ₹ 4,50,000

(ii) Net Working Capital = Current Assets – Current Liabilities
= 4,50,000 – 3,60,000
= ₹ 90,000

1.4 KINDS OF WORKING CAPITAL

The working capital may be classified on the basis of:

1. Concept
2. Time

1. On the Basis of Concept: On the basis of concept, working capital may be classified as:

(i) Gross Working Capital
(ii) Net Working Capital

2. On the Basis of Time: On the basis of time, working capital may be classified as:

(a) Permanent or Fixed Working Capital
(b) Temporary or Variable Working Capital

(a) Permanent or Fixed Working Capital: As the name indicates, Permanent or Fixed Working Capital is that type of working capital which is permanently blocked in current assets. Therefore, it is referred as core working capital. In other words, it is the minimum level of current assets which is to be maintained all the time in the business for effective utilisation of fixed facilities and to operate the business activities properly. If the minimum level is not maintained then it may lead to blocking of circulation of capital. This working capital may vary in proportion to the growth of business. Thus, increases with increase in the size of the business. For financing of permanent working capital, generally, long-term funds are used. It may be further classified as:

(i) Regular Working Capital
(ii) Reserve Working Capital

(i) Regular Working Capital: The regular working capital is needed to ensure the smooth running of operating cycle. The need of current assets is required constantly, i.e., from cash to inventories, inventory to sales, sales to debtors and debtors to cash.

(ii) Reserve Working Capital: The reserve working capital is that which is over and above the regular working capital requirement and maintained in the business. In other words, it is the capital which is used for meeting any contingencies like rise in prices of material or other inputs. It is the conservative approach from the point of view of the finance manager who does not want to take any risk when exigencies arise. Thus, the reserve working capital provide a cushion to finance manager to play safe.

(b) Temporary or Variable Working Capital: The business may also need additional working capital to meet seasonal demands and special needs. This is the extra working capital which is needed on account of changes in the activities or volume of the business, i.e., increase in production due to more demand of the product in the market, arrangement of additional inputs, etc. Temporary working capital meets the liquidity requirements of the firm. This may be further classified in two categories:

(i) Seasonal Working Capital
(ii) Special Working Capital

(i) Seasonal Working Capital: It is the capital which is needed to meet the seasonal demands and unanticipated conditions like festival demand, competition in the market, support sales during the peak period, etc.

(ii) Special Working Capital: The special working capital is required to support the extraordinary needs or special contingencies like launching of special advertising campaigning, special demand of the market, etc.

The difference between the permanent and temporary working capital has been depicted with the help of the graphs [Figure 1.1(a) and Figure 1.1(b)]:

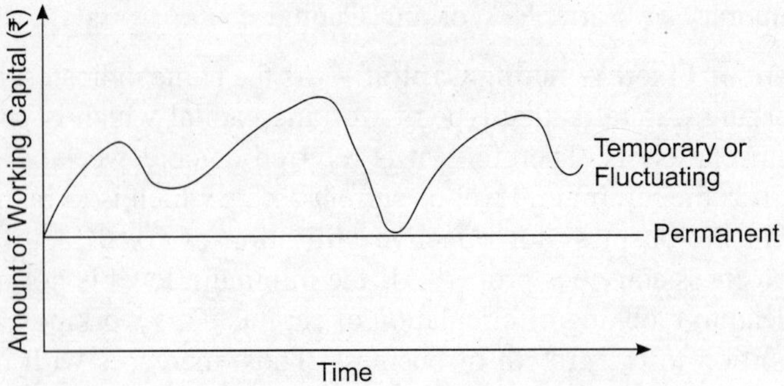

FIGURE 1.1(a) When the firm is stable.

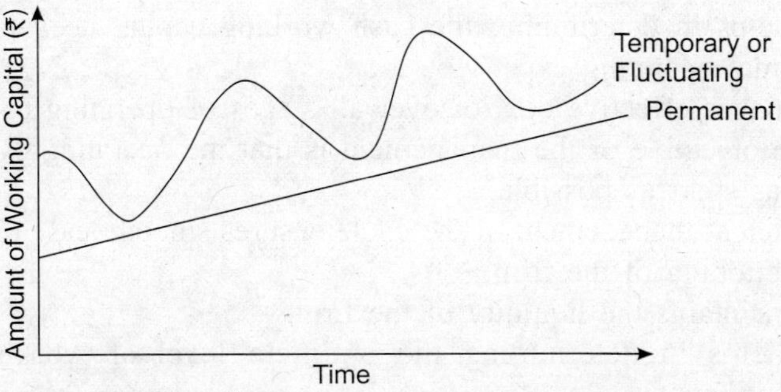

FIGURE 1.1(b) When the firm is growing.

Graph in Figure 1.1(a) shows that permanent working capital is stable over a period of time while variable working capital is fluctuating. This is the situation of the stable firm. In case of the growing firm, the Graph in Figure 1.1(b) shows that the permanent working capital is increasing during the passage of time while variable working capital is fluctuating, i.e., increasing or decreasing during the passage of time.

1.5 OPERATING CYCLE CONCEPT OF WORKING CAPITAL

Operating Cycle concept of the working capital explains the practical side of the working capital management. In a manufacturing organisation, it starts from the purchase of raw material and conversion of raw material into work-in-progress and finished goods. Further, finished goods are converted into credit sales resulting into creation of accounts receivables and these are converted into cash. Thus, operating cycle refers to the average time duration between acquisition of raw materials and the final cash realisation. In other words, it is also said as cash-to-cash conversion cycle. The operating cycle of a manufacturing firm consists of six stages:

(i) Acquisition of raw material stage
(ii) Conversion of raw material into work-in-progress stage
(iii) Conversion of work-in-progress into finished goods stage
(iv) Conversion of finished goods into sales stage
(v) Creation of account receivables stage
(vi) Receivable stage to cash stage

The operating cycle of working capital has been depicted in the Figure 1.2.

1.5.1 Importance of Operating Cycle

The operating cycle concept of working capital is gaining more and more importance from the practical utility point of view because it gives emphasis on all the stages of cash-to-cash conversion cycle. The importance of the concept is as follows:

(i) It helps in determining the cash working capital need to meet the normal operating expenses.

(ii) It makes effective control over all stages of operating cycle.

(iii) The objective of the management is that the operating cycle should be as short as possible.

(iv) Efficient management of the cycle ensures smooth and uninterrupted functioning of the firm.

(v) It maintains the liquidity of the firm.

(vi) It helps in determining the optimum level of working capital requirement.

(vii) The length of operating cycle shows the performance of operating management. If the cycle is short, it shows efficient management of different components of working capital and vice-versa.

(viii) The length of net operating cycle is the indicator of the requirement of the working capital during the period for which the finance manager has to make arrangement of funds either from internal sources or external sources, i.e., Bank.

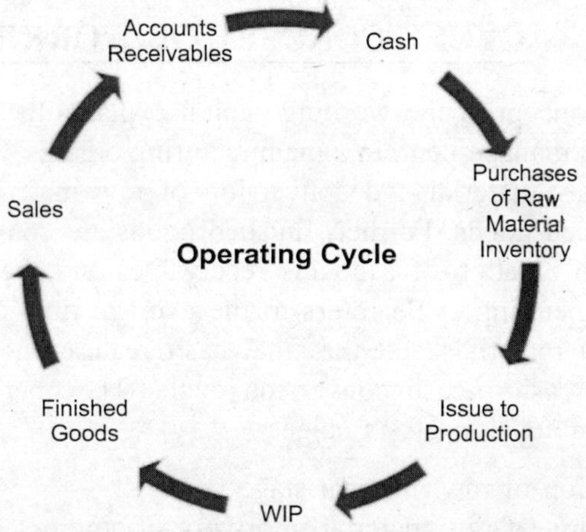

FIGURE 1.2 Operating cycle of working capital.

1.5.2 Types of Operating Cycle

The operating cycle may be classified under two categories from the point of view of computation:

1. **Gross Operating Cycle:** It is the aggregate of Raw Material Conversion Period (RMCP), Work-in-progress Conversion Period (WIPCP), Finished Goods Conversion Period (FGCP) and Book Debts Conversion Period (BDCP). This can be represented with the help of the following equation:

   Gross Operating Cycle = RMCP + WIPCP + FGCP + BDCP

2. **Net Operating Cycle:** Generally, firm extends credit facilities to customers for increasing sales and, at the same time, firm receives the credit in purchasing of materials from suppliers. The credit period extended to the firm by the suppliers is known as payment deferral period (PDP). This payment deferral period affects the operating cycle positively by reducing the period of operating cycle. Net operating cycle is also known as cash-to-cash conversion cycle. Net operating cycle may be expressed with the help of the following equation:

Net Operating Cycle = Gross Operating Cycle
– Payment Deferral Period (PDP)

ILLUSTRATION 1.2: The following information has been obtained from the books of a manufacturing company:

Particulars	*Year*	
	2020	*2021*
	Amount (₹)	*Amount* (₹)
Raw materials inventory	90,000	1,02,000
Work-in-progress	62,500	72,500
Finished goods stock	60,000	80,000
Sales	6,80,000	7,80,000
Debtors	1,36,000	1,47,000
Creditors	65,000	75,000
Cost of Goods sold	6,00,000	7,00,000
Purchases	4,25,000	4,51,000
Consumption of raw materials	4,11,000	4,39,000

Calculate:

(i) Gross Operating Cycle
(ii) Net Operating Cycle
(iii) Number of Operating Cycle
(iv) Amount of Working Capital per Operating Cycle

Solution:

(i) Gross Operating Cycle

(a) Raw Material Conversion Period (RMCP)

$$= \frac{\text{Average Value of Raw Material Stock}}{\text{Average Consumption of Raw Material}} \times 365$$

$$= \frac{96,000}{4,25,000} \times 365$$

= 82 days

(b) WIP Conversion Period (WIPCP)

$$= \frac{\text{Average Work-in-Progress}}{\text{Average Cost of Goods Sold}} \times 365$$

$$= \frac{67,500}{6,50,000} \times 365$$

= 38 days

(c) Finished Goods Conversion Period (FGCP)

$$= \frac{\text{Average Finished Goods Stock}}{\text{Average Cost of Goods Sold}} \times 365$$

$$= \frac{70,000}{6,50,000} \times 365$$

= 39 days

(d) Book Debts Conversion Period (BDCP)

$$= \frac{\text{Average Value of Debtors}}{\text{Average Value of Sales}} \times 365$$

$$= \frac{1,41,500}{7,30,000} \times 365$$

= 71 days

Gross Operating Cycle = RMCP + WIPCP + FGCP + BDCP
= 82 + 38 + 39 + 71 = 230 days

(ii) Net Operating Cycle

Payment Deferral Period (PDP)

$$= \frac{\text{Average Value of Creditors}}{\text{Average Purchase of Raw Materials}} \times 365$$

$$= \frac{70,000}{4,38,000} \times 365$$

= 58 days

Net Operating Cycle = Gross Operating Cycle – Payment Deferral Period
= 230 – 58 =172 days

(iii) Number of Operating Cycle $= \frac{\text{Days in a Year}}{\text{One Operating Cycle Period}}$

$$= \frac{365}{172}$$

= 2.12 cycles

(iv) Amount of Working Capital per Cycle

$$= \frac{\text{Total Operating Cost}}{\text{No. of Operating Cycle in a Year}}$$

$$= \frac{7,00,000}{2.12}$$

= ₹ 3,30,189

Working Notes:

				₹
Average Raw Material Inventory	=	(90,000 + 1,02,000)/2	=	96,000
Average Work-in-progress	=	(62,500 + 72,500)/2	=	67,500
Average Finished Goods stock	=	(60,000 + 80,000)/2	=	70,000
Average Sales	=	(6,80,000 + 7,80,000)/2	=	7,30,000
Average Debtors	=	(1,36,000 + 1,47,000)/2	=	1,41,500
Average Creditors	=	(65,000 + 75,000)/2	=	70,000
Average Cost of Goods sold	=	(6,00,000 + 7,00,000)/2	=	6,50,000
Average Purchases	=	(4,25,000 + 4,51,000)/2	=	4,38,000
Average Consumption of Raw Materials	=	(4,11,000 + 4,39,000)/2	=	4,25,000

1.6 NATURE OF WORKING CAPITAL

The capital of the firm may be classified under two categories—Fixed Capital and Variable Capital. Fixed capital is used for meeting long-term requirements, i.e., financing of fixed assets while variable capital is used for meeting short-term requirements, i.e., not more than a year. In other words, variable capital is also termed as working capital, current capital or trading capital which is used for meeting operational aspects of the business, i.e., purchasing of raw materials, meeting day-to-day expenses, etc. According to J. H. Bonnevile and L. E. Dewey, "The capital invested therein represents a sort of revolving fund, starting with cash that is used to pay for raw material, labour and other operating expenses and that is to be recovered again through the sale of finished product." The nature of working capital is the liquid investment. The fund invested in the form of working capital is realised within a year from the conversion of components of current assets into cash. In this way, the working capital changes its face from one form to another form during the normal business operations. The value of current assets does not depreciate as in case of fixed assets. The working capital makes the use of fixed facilities efficiently.

1.7 NEED FOR WORKING CAPITAL

The basic objective of financial management is to increase or maximise shareholders' wealth without increasing the riskiness (liability) of the business.

This is only possible when the business earns sufficient profits which is based on the size of the sales. This all requires the efficient management of working capital which will ensure efficient utilisation of fixed facilities as well as current facilities. In the operating cycle, there is a time gap among the activities, i.e., conversion of raw materials into finished goods, conversion of finished goods into sales and creation of book debts and lastly, conversion of book debts into cash. Because of these conversion periods, a firm has to make arrangement of working capital all the time in the business for smooth running and meeting day-to-day expenses and any contingencies of the business. A new firm needs the working capital on regular basis because it is unable to generate cash in short period. Therefore, it has to make arrangement from external sources, i.e., bank or financial institutions to meet out any deficit of working capital. On the contrary, a growing firm needs the larger amount of working capital to meet the growing needs of the business. Hence, the role of finance manager is to keep a watchful eye on the availability of external and internal sources to avoid any deficit of working capital. After growing stage, a firm moves to maturity stage where it requires normal working capital so that finance manager could run the business smoothly. Thus, the need for maintaining an adequate working capital is essential for the firm. Its need should be accurately estimated from time to time. In view of the above, all types of firms need the working capital for the following requirements:

(i) Purchase of raw materials and other stores.
(ii) Payment of wages and salaries.
(iii) Payment of day-to-day expenses.
(iv) To meet all overheads costs like factory, office and selling overheads.
(v) To extend credit facilities to customers through credit sales.
(vi) To maintain minimum stock of raw materials for smooth running of production process.
(vii) To maintain sufficient stock of finished goods for regular and spontaneous demand of the product in the market and to meet the competition successfully.
(viii) To meet the need of external economic environment on account of price trend, credit policy of the Central Bank, Government policy, etc.

1.8 OBJECTIVES OF WORKING CAPITAL

Working capital is the lifeblood for any organisation. It runs the business activities properly. The objective of the working capital, generally, is to provide funds to business as and when needed. The following are the objectives of working capital:

1. To increase the shareholders' wealth by proper management of working capital, i.e., current assets and current liabilities.

2. To ensure minimum locking of funds in the different components of current assets.
3. To make the payment of current liabilities in time so that suppliers' credit could be availed regularly.
4. The current assets should be managed efficiently so that return on current assets should be more than the cost.
5. To ensure regular supply of raw materials to the production.
6. To ensure efficient utilisation of fixed facilities.
7. To make availability of funds to the various business operations timely.
8. To meet the seasonal and special needs of the business.

1.9 FACTORS INFLUENCING WORKING CAPITAL NEED

There is no thumb rule for ascertaining working capital need of a firm accurately. Needs are affected by the internal and external environment, nature of business, stage in business operations, etc. The factors which are influencing working capital needs also determine the total investment in working capital from time to time. The following are the significant factors which are generally influencing the working capital requirements:

1.9.1 Nature of Business

(i) The nature of business may be trading organisation, manufacturing organisation, service organisation and public utilities organisation.

(ii) The requirement of working capital will be different in above mentioned organisations due to nature of functioning and investment in fixed assets and current assets.

(iii) In case of trading organisation, a large sum will be required for maintaining the large stocks of variety of merchandised. In addition to this, the working capital will also be invested in receivables due to credit facilities provided to customers and cash balance. On the other hand, a small amount will also be required for investment in fixed facilities for running the business.

(iv) In case of manufacturing organisation, substantial amount of working capital for inputs is required all the time to keep the production process uninterrupted. In addition to this, the investment in fixed assets is also needed in significant quantity.

(v) In case of transport organisations, major part of the funds is invested in fixed assets like Buses, Trucks, Cars, etc. The current fund will be required for running these services. Therefore, working capital requirement will be nominal because they offer cash services mainly.

(vi) In case of public utilities undertakings like Electricity, Railways, etc. large funds are invested in fixed assets. They need a limited working capital because they also offer cash services generally.

1.9.2 Size of Business

(i) The size of business also plays a significant role in determining the need of working capital. Size may be decided in terms of scale of operations.
(ii) If the scale of operation is higher, the firm will need more working capital.
(iii) In contrast, the firm having small scale of operations will need less amount of working capital.
(iv) However, in small firms, where turnover rate is slow, the large sum will be locked up in inventories, high overhead charges, etc., will need more amount of working capital.

1.9.3 Manufacturing Cycle

(i) Manufacturing cycle represents time span required for conversion of raw materials into finished products.
(ii) The length of manufacturing cycle determines the requirement of working capital.
(iii) The longer the manufacturing cycle, large sum of the working capital will be required and vice-versa.
(iv) An extended manufacturing cycle refers that a large sum will be locked up in inventories.
(v) Thus, adherence to the manufacturing cycle is needed for keeping the working capital requirement at minimum or optimum level.

1.9.4 Production Policy

(i) Generally, the firm maintains a regular production policy to meet the demand of the product in the market.
(ii) Seasonal factors affect the production schedule of any organisation.
(iii) In off season, if steady production policy is adopted, it will lead to high demand of working capital due to accumulation of inventories (finished goods). The purpose of keeping stock is to meet high demand in season, e.g., woollen garments in the winter season.
(iv) In peak season, large amount of working capital will be needed to meet the extra demand of the market, e.g., festival season.

1.9.5 Seasonal Variations

(i) Seasonal factors encourage for the accumulation of inventories.
(ii) In certain industries raw materials are not available all the time such as sugarcane, mustard oil seeds, etc.
(iii) In such situation, the high amount of working capital is required for the storage of raw materials.

1.9.6 Working Capital Cycle

(i) The working capital cycle refers to the time elapses between the purchase of raw material to finished goods and finished goods to receivables and conversion of receivables into cash. In other words, it is also called cash to cash conversion cycle.

(ii) The length of working capital cycle determines the size of working capital.

(iii) The longer the period of cycle larger the amount of working capital and vice-versa.

(iv) Thus, in order to keep the amount of working capital at optimum or minimum level, the management has to put extra efforts in reducing the period of cycle.

1.9.7 Price Level Changes

(i) Price level changes also affect the requirement of working capital in some industries where raw materials are available in season only or cheaper in season.

(ii) During price rising more amount of working capital will be needed to maintain the same level of investment in current assets.

(iii) Companies which can revise the price of their products with the increase in the price of raw materials, will not have much problem for working capital.

(iv) Thus, the finance manager should keep a watchful eye on the price fluctuations of materials in the market to minimise its effect on the working capital.

1.9.8 Credit Policy of the Firm

(i) Credit policy means dealing with debtors or extending credit to customers.

(ii) The credit policy may not be same for all customers. It depends upon the creditworthiness of individual customers.

(iii) Generally, two types of credit policies are followed by the organisation either strict or liberal.

(iv) Liberal credit policy may lead to the collection problem which may be in the form of high collection period. In such situation large amount of working capital will be required and the chances of bad debts may increase.

(v) On the other hand, strict credit policy size up the creditworthiness of individual customer before granting the credit. In such situation, the collection of debt will be in time hence, less amount of working capital will be needed. At the same time chances of bad debts will also be minimum. But it may adversely affect the size of sales.

(vi) Thus, it may be said that the credit policy should be moderate so that it should not affect the business adversely.

1.9.9 Frequency of Stock Turnover

(i) The objective of every organisation is to increase the profit which is possible by increasing the rate of stock turnover or sales.
(ii) If the frequency of stock turnover is high, the firm will need lower amount of working capital because of conversion of sales into cash at a faster speed.
(iii) In contrary, firm having low sales growth will need higher amount of working capital.
(iv) The firms having business of precious metals and stones will require higher amount of working capital due to slow movement of stock.

1.9.10 Business Cycle

(i) This is another factor which also affects the need of working capital.
(ii) During the economic boom period large amount of working capital is needed due to increase in sales, rise in prices, expansion of business.
(iii) In contrary, during the recession period or down swing period sales declines and slow economic activities adversely affect the business of the firm resulting into less requirement of working capital.

1.9.11 Rate of Growth and Diversification of Business

(i) Growth in business also affects the quantum of working capital.
(ii) In case of normal growth, the requirement of working capital may be met from internal sources, i.e., retained profits. Therefore, less working capital will be needed.
(iii) In case of fast growth, large amount of working capital will be needed due to size of scale of operations.
(iv) Diversification of business calls for larger amount of working capital. In such situation, the management has to assess the need in advance so that the diversification policy could be smoothly implemented.

1.9.12 Credit Availability

(i) It is a common practice that every organisation purchases raw materials and other inputs on credit and suppliers give credit to the purchaser. The period, for which the credit is given, is known as payment deferral period.
(ii) The length of payment deferral period affects the quantum of working capital.
(iii) If liberal credit terms are available from the suppliers, the less amount of working capital will be needed and vice-versa.

(iv) Similarly, banks also extend credit facilities on favourable terms and conditions depending upon the creditworthiness of the firm and payment of debt in time. In such situation, the firm may operate with less working capital due to good relations with financial institutions.

1.9.13 Operating Performance

(i) Operating performance directly affects the earning capacity of the firm.
(ii) Operating efficiency means optimum utilisation of resources which minimises the operating cost and increase profitability position of the firm.
(iii) If operating efficiency is good, the firm may contribute from internal sources to its working capital requirements.

1.9.14 Economic Factors

(i) Economic factors like banking facilities, import policy, irregularity of supply, stability in money market, etc., also affect business performance and working capital requirements accordingly.
(ii) If economic factors are favourable to the business, less amount of working capital will be required by the firm and vice-versa.

1.9.15 Management Attitude

(i) The management attitude, ability and efficiency also have considerable impact on the estimation of working capital requirement.
(ii) If the attitude of the management is conservative, more working capital will be required in the business due to risk averse approach.
(iii) If the attitude of the management is aggressive, less working capital will be maintained in the business due to good relationship with the financial institutions. This will help in obtaining funds in short period in case of exigencies. Such type of attitude of the management is ready to take risk.
(iv) Management policies regarding payment of cash dividend, flexible capital structure, stock reserves, etc., will also influence the working capital need.

1.10 ESTIMATING WORKING CAPITAL NEEDS

Working capital needs are estimated for the ensuing year. In order to avoid any deficiency in working capital, an estimate of working capital should be made in advance. The basic purpose is to measure the cash position of the firm and to exercise effective control over the liquidity position of the firm.

1.11 TECHNIQUES OF ESTIMATING WORKING CAPITAL NEED

Generally, the techniques which are used in estimating working capital need are:

1. Estimation of different Components of Working Capital Method
2. Percentage of Sales Method
3. Regression Analysis Technique
4. Operating Cycle Method

1. **Estimation of Different Components of Working Capital Method:** There are two concepts of working Capital—Gross and Net working capital. Under this method a forecast is made of different constituents of current assets and current liabilities. Therefore, this method is also called Balance Sheet Method. The aggregate of current assets will show the gross working capital requirement while the difference between current assets and current liabilities will show net working capital requirement. The difference will indicate either cash surplus (positive working capital) or cash deficiency (negative working capital).

Estimation of Different Constituents of Current Assets

A. Inventories: The term inventories include mainly stock of raw materials, work-in-progress and stock of finished goods.

(a) **Stock of raw materials:** The investment in raw materials shall be decided on the basis of holding period, adjustment for contingencies and seasonal factors. The holding period shall be based upon replenishment period of fresh delivery.
(b) **Work-in-progress:** The work-in-progress shall be decided on the basis of average time period for which inputs will be in the process of production. The inputs are raw materials, wages and overheads.
(c) **Stock of finished goods:** The conversion of finished goods into sales takes some time and kept in warehouse. This conversion period is important because the investment in finished goods will be locked during that period.

B. Debtors: Debtors are outcome of credit sales. The amount of debtor will be based on the size of credit sales, credit period allowed and efficiency in realisation of debtors.

C. Cash and Bank Balance: The cash and bank balances are generally based on the basis of past performance or experience. The attitude of management towards taking risk also plays a significant role in estimating the amount of cash and bank balances. Similarly, the relationship of finance manager with the financial institutions also affects the amount of these balances. It ensures access of borrowing in time of need or exigencies.

Estimation of Different Constituents of Current Liabilities

(a) **Sundry Creditors:** Sundry creditors are estimated on the basis of credit purchases and the credit period allowed by suppliers.
(b) **Outstanding Expenses:** The amount of outstanding expenses, i.e., salaries, wages and other expenses are estimated on the basis of lag in payment.

ILLUSTRATION 1.3: The Jai Brothers Ltd. wants to purchase a business and seeks your advice about the average amount of working capital which will be required in the first year of working. You are also instructed to assume a 10% safety margin. Ascertain the requirement of working capital. Its annual figures are as follows:

		₹
(i)	Stock of raw materials	4,50,000
(ii)	Stock of finished goods	13,50,000
(iii)	Inland sales–at one month's credit	12,00,000
(iv)	Export sales–at three month's credit	4,50,000
(v)	Wages paid–half month arrears	2,40,000
(vi)	Manufacturing overheads paid–one month arrear	1,80,000
(vii)	Administration overheads paid–one month arrear	4,80,000
(viii)	Sales promotion expenses paid quarterly in advance	3,20,000
(ix)	Materials used–supplier extended two month's credit	3,60,000
(x)	Cash	50,000
(xi)	Bank balance	1,00,000

The company keeps one month's stock each of raw materials and finished goods. Ignore work-in-progress.

Solution:

Statement of Working Capital Requirements

Current Assets:

		₹
Stock of raw materials	4,50,000 × 1/12	37,500
Stock of finished goods	13,50,000 × 1/12	1,12,500
Book Debts:		
Inland Sales	12,00,000 × 1/12	1,00,000
Export Sales	4,50,000 × 3/12	1,12,500
Prepaid Sales Promotion		3,20,000
Cash		50,000
Bank balance		1,00,000
	Investment in Current Assets or Gross Working Capital	8,32,500

Current Liabilities:

Lag in payments:		
Wages	2,40,000 × 1/12 × 1/2	10,000
Manufacturing Overheads	1,80,000 × 1/12	15,000
Administration Overheads	4,80,000 × 1/12	40,000
Creditors	3,60,000 × 2/12	60,000
	Investment in Current Liabilities	1,25,000

Net Working Capital = 8,32,500 – 1,25,000
= 7,07,500

Add 10% for Safety Margin 70,750
Average amount of working Capital = ₹ 7,78,250

By Determining Cash Cost of Current Assets and Current Liabilities

In this case, the cash cost involved in the current assets will be considered. Cash cost does not involve any margin of profit and other expenses. In this approach debtors are computed as a percentage of cash cost not as a percentage of sales. This is the aggressive approach of estimating the working capital need. Thus, the working capital needs are calculated taking into account cash cost locked in sundry debtors, work-in-progress and finished goods.

Cash Cost = Sales – (Profit Margin + Other Expenses)

The objective of this approach is that the company has to receive production cost instead of total cost which includes profit margin. For example, if the debtors are estimated ₹ 1,25,000 and cost of production is ₹ 1,00,000 then the amount of funds locked with them are ₹ 1,00,000 only instead of ₹ 1,25,000.

ILLUSTRATION 1.4: The Directors of Alpha Beta Ltd. sells its products in domestic market at a gross profit of 20%. Depreciation is taken into account as a part of cost of production. The following data are available for the year 2022:

	₹
Sales (two month's credit)	18,50,000
Materials used (one month credit)	6,00,000
Wages (half month lag in payment)	4,80,000
Cash manufacturing expenses (one month lag in payment)	3,40,000
Administration overheads (one month lag in payment)	1,20,000
Sales promotion expenses payable quarterly in advance	1,20,000

The company maintains raw materials stock for one month and finished goods stock for two months. The cash in hand is maintained ₹ 50,000. You are required to calculate:

(i) Total manufacturing expenses
(ii) Amount of depreciation
(iii) Total cash cost of debtors
(iv) Working capital requirement

Solution:

(i) Total Manufacturing Expense:

			₹
Sales			18,50,000
Less: Gross profit			3,70,000
	Cost of sales		14,80,000
Less: Cost of material		6,00,000	
Wages		4,80,000	10,80,000
	Total manufacturing expenses		4,00,000

(ii) Depreciation:

Total manufacturing expenses		4,00,000
Less: Cash manufacturing expenses		3,40,000
	Depreciation	60,000

(iii) Cash Cost of Debtors:

Total manufacturing cost			14,80,000
Less: Depreciation			60,000
	Cost of Production		14,20,000
Add: Administration overheads		1,20,000	
Sales promotion		30,000	1,50,000
	Cost of sales		15,70,000

(iv) Statement of Working Capital Requirement

A. Current Assets		Sales Basis ₹	Cash Cost Basis ₹
Raw material	6,00,000 × 1/12	50,000	50,000
Finished goods	14,20,000 × 2/12	2,36,667	2,36,667
Debtors:			
Sales	18,50,000 × 2/12	3,08,333	
Cash Cost	15,70,000 × 2/12	2,61,667	
Sales promotion expenses	1,20,000 × 3/12	30,000	30,000
Cash	50,000	50,000	
	6,75,000	6,28,334	
B. Current Liabilities			
Creditors	6,00,000 × 1/12	50,000	50,000
Wages	4,80,000 × 0.5/12	20,000	20,000
Manufacturing expenses	3,40,000 × 1/12	28,333	28,333
Administration overhead	1,20,000 × 1/12	10,000	10,000
	1,08,333	1,08,333	
Working Capital (A–B)	5,66,667	5,20,001	

2. Percentage of Sales Method: This is a simple and traditional method of determining the working capital requirement. It is computed on the basis of percentage of sales. Percentage of sales is decided on the basis of past experience. For example, if the percentage of sales is 20% and sales are ₹ 2,00,000 then working capital would be ₹ 40,000. The different constituents of current assets and current liabilities are determined on the basis of percentage of sales. This method is useful when sales and working capital relation is stable. It is useful for projecting short-term changes in working capital. The method attracts the criticism on the basis of that it presumes linear relationship between sales and working capital which is not applicable in all cases. Therefore, the method does not assume any practical application.

ILLUSTRATION 1.5: The Balance Sheet of Sudarshan Ltd. for the year ending 31st March, 2022 is as follows:

Balance Sheet of Sudarshan Ltd. as on 31st March, 2022

Liabilities	*Amount* ₹	*Assets*	*Amount* ₹
Share capital	12,00,000	Land and Building	3,00,000
Reserve and Surplus	6,00,000	Plant and Machinery	8,00,000
Profit and Loss A/c	2,00,000	Furniture and Fixtures	2,00,000
Long-term loans	10,00,000	Stock of Finished Goods	12,00,000
Debentures	2,00,000	Debtors	10,00,000
Creditors	8,00,000	Bills Receivables	5,00,000
Overdraft	1,00,000	Cash	1,00,000
Bills Payable	2,00,000	Bank Balance	2,00,000
	43,00,000		43,00,000

The company's Turnover for the year 2020–21 was ₹ 50 lakh. It is anticipated that sales will become double in the year 2021–2022. You are required to estimate the working capital requirement of Sudarshan Ltd. for the year 2021–2022:

Solution:

Estimation of working Capital Requirement for the year 2021–2022

Particulars	*% of sales based on 2020–21*	*2020–21 Actual*	*2021–22 Estimates*
Sales		₹	₹
	100	50,00,000	100,00,000
A. Current Assets			
Stock of finished goods	24	12,00,000	24,00,000
Debtors	20	10,00,000	20,00,000
Bills receivables	10	5,00,000	10,00,000
Cash	02	1,00,000	2,00,000
Bank balance	04	2,00,000	4.00.000
Total	60	30,00,000	60,00,000
B. Current Liabilities			
Creditors	16	8,00,000	16,00,000
Overdraft	02	1,00,000	2,00,000
Bills payable	04	2,00,000	4,00,000
Total	22	11,00,000	22,00,000
Working Capital (A–B)	38	19,00,000	38,00,000

3. Regression Analysis: It is a statistical technique which can also be used for estimating working capital requirement. It establishes relationship between sales and working capital and its various components. The method of Least-Square is used. It is as follows:

If

Sales = x

Working Capital = y

The relationship between x and y is expressed with the help of the following equations:

$Y = a + bx$

$\sum y = na + b\sum x$

$\sum xy = a\sum x + b\sum x^2$

Where:

a = Fixed Component

b = Variable Component

n = No. of Observations

ILLUSTRATION 1.6: The following information are available of Kanji Lal Ltd. for the period of five years of sales and current assets:

Year	Sales (x) ₹ in lakh	Current Assets (y) ₹ in lakh
2018	16	11
2019	22	14
2020	26	16
2021	28	22
2022	35	23

Estimate working capital requirement for the year 2023 if anticipated sales are ₹ 44 lakh.

Solution:

Year	*Sales* (x)	*Current assets* (y)	xy	x^2
2018	16	11	176	256
2019	22	14	308	484
2020	26	16	416	676
2021	28	22	616	784
2022	35	23	805	1225
	$\sum x = 127$	$\sum y = 86$	$\sum xy = 2321$	$\sum x^2 = 3425$

$$\sum y = na + b\sum x$$

$$86 = 5a + 127b \quad (1)$$

$$\sum xy = a\sum x + b\sum x^2$$

$$2321 = 127a + 3425b \quad (2)$$

By solving the equations (1) and (2)

$a = -0.072$ $b = 0.68$

Working Capital:

$$y = a + bx$$
$$y = -0.072 + 0.68 \times 44$$
$$y = 29.848$$

or Gross working Capital = ₹ 29.848 lakh for the year 2023.

4. Operating Cycle Method: The operating cycle method may be used under the following approach:

A. Total operating cycle period
B. Individual components of operating cycle

A. Total operating cycle period: Under this approach, working capital estimate is done for one operating cycle period. The following formula is used:

$$\text{Working Capital} = \frac{\text{Estimated cost of goods sold}}{365} \times \text{Operating cycle period} + \text{Desired Cash balance}$$

ILLUSTRATION 1.7: The cost of goods sold of a manufacturing company is ₹ 3,65,00,000. The expected operating cycle period is 73 days. Cash in hand and at bank is expected to be ₹ 70,000. Number of days in a year are 365. Compute the working capital requirement.

Solution:

$$\text{Working Capital} = \frac{\text{Estimated cost of goods}}{365} \times \text{Operating cycle period} + \text{Desired cash}$$

$$= \frac{3,65,00,000}{365} \times 73 + 70,000$$

$$= 73,00,000 + 70,000 = ₹\ 73,70,000$$

B. Individual components of operating cycle: Under this approach, estimation of working capital is done by determining the individual components of operating cycle, i.e., raw materials, work-in-progress, finished goods, debtors, creditors and lag in payment of expenses. The following illustration explains this concept:

ILLUSTRATION 1.8: The Board of Directors of Snowwhite Ltd. requests you to prepare a statement of working capital requirement to finance a level of activity of 1,56,000 units of production. A proforma Cost Sheet of the company provides the following information:

		₹
Raw materials		70
Direct wages		40
Overheads		50
	Total Cost	160
	Profit	40
	Selling Price	200

Further Information:

(i)	Raw materials in stock	4 weeks
(ii)	Finished goods in stock	4 weeks
(iii)	Materials in process	2 weeks
(iv)	Credit allowed by suppliers	4 weeks
(v)	Credit allowed to customers	6 weeks
(vi)	Lag in payment of wages	2 weeks
(vii)	Lag in payment of overheads	4 weeks
(viii)	20% output sold in cash	
(ix)	Cash in hand and at bank is expected to be ₹ 50,000.	
(x)	Add 10% to your estimated figure to cover unforeseen contingencies.	
(xi)	A time period of four weeks is equivalent to a month.	
(xii)	Assume that production is carried out evenly throughout the year.	
(xiii)	Assume 50% completion stage as regards wages and overheads.	

Solution:

Statement of Working Capital Requirement

A. Current Assets:

			₹
Raw materials	$\frac{1,56,000}{52} \times 4 \times 70$		8,40,000
Work-in-progress	$\frac{1,56,000}{52} \times 2$		
No. of units	= 6,000 units		
Raw materials	6,000 × 70	4,20,000	
Wages	6,000 × 40 × 1/2	1,20,000	
Overheads	6,000 × 50 × 1/2	1,50,000	6,90,000
Finished goods	$\frac{1,56,000}{52} \times 4 \times 160$		19,20,000
Debtors	$\frac{1,56,000}{52} \times 6 \times 160 \times \frac{80}{100}$		23,04,000
Cash in hand and at Bank			50,000
			58,04,000

B. Current Liabilities:

		₹
Creditors	$\frac{1,56,000}{52} \times 4 \times 70$	8,40,000
Wages payable	$\frac{1,56,000}{52} \times 2 \times 40$	2,40,000

Overheads payable	$\frac{1,56,000}{52} \times 4 \times 50$	6,00,000
		16,80,000
Net Working Capital (A–B)		41,24,000
Add: 10% for Contingencies		4,12,400
Total Working Capital Requirement		45,36,400

ILLUSTRATION 1.9: A newly established company commencing business in 2021. The company wishes to know the amount of working capital which will be needed to meet the programme of activity they have planned for the year. The company provides the following information:

(i) Level of activity per annum 1,56,000 units
(ii) Weeks in a year 52
(iii) Selling price ₹ 200 per unit
(iv) Cost of material ₹ 40 per unit
(v) Cost of labour ₹ 15 per unit
(vi) Overheads ₹ 30 per unit
(vii) Raw material in stock (One month)
(viii) Production process (Half month)
(ix) Finished goods in stock (One month)
(x) Credit allowed by suppliers (Six weeks)
(xi) Credit given to customers (Eight weeks)
(xii) Lag in payment of wages (Two weeks)
(xiii) Lag in payment of overheads (Two weeks)
(xiv) Cash at Bank ₹ 50,000

25% output is sold on cash basis. You are required to prepare a statement in columnar form showing the working capital requirement in total and as regards each constituent of current assets and current liabilities. Work-in-process may be assumed to be 100% complete regards material and 50% as regards labour and overheads.

Solution:

Statement of Working Capital Requirement

Particulars	*Period in weeks*	*Total ₹*	*Raw Materials ₹*	*Work-in-process ₹*	*Finished Goods ₹*	*Debtors ₹*	*Cash at Bank ₹*
A. Current Assets							
1. Raw Materials							
(a) Stock	4		4,80,000				
(b) Work-in-process	2			2,40,000			
(c) Finished Goods	4				4,80,000		
(d) Debtors	8					7,20,000	
Sub-total	**18**	**19,20,000**					

(Contd.)

Particulars	*Period in weeks*	*Total ₹*	*Raw Materials ₹*	*Work-in-process ₹*	*Finished Goods ₹*	*Debtors ₹*	*Cash at Bank ₹*
2. Labour							
(a) Work-in-process	1			45,000			
(b) Finished goods	4				1,80,000		
(c) Debtors	8					2,70,000	
Sub-total	**13**	**4,95,000**					
3. Overheads							
(a) Work-in-process	1			90,000			
(b) Finished Goods	4				3,60,000		
(c) Debtors	8					5,40,000	
Sub-total	**13**	**9,90,000**					
4. Cash at Bank		50,000					50,000
Total Current Assets		**34,55,000**	**4,80,000**	**3,75,000**	**10,20,000**	**15,30,000**	**50,000**

B. Current Liabilities	*Period in weeks*	*Total ₹*	*Raw Materials ₹*	*Wages ₹*	*Overheads ₹*
5. Credit by Suppliers	6	7,20,000	7,20,000		
6. Lag in payment of wages	2	90,000		90,000	
7. Lag in payment of overheads	2	1,80,000			1,80,000
Total Current Liabilities	**10**	**9,90,000**	**7,20,000**	**90,000**	**1,80,000**
Working Capital (A-B)		**24,65,000**			

Working Notes:

1. Weekly Output $1,56,000/52 = 3,000$ units

2. Raw Materials

			₹
(a) In stock	$3,000 \times 4 \times 40$	=	4,80,000
(b) In work-in-process	$3,000 \times 2 \times 40$	=	2,40,000
(c) In finished goods	$3,000 \times 4 \times 40$	=	4,80,000
(d) In credit to debtors	$\frac{3,000 \times 8 \times 40 \times 75}{100}$	=	7,20,000
			19,20,000

3. Labour			
(a) In work-in-process	3,000 × 15 × 1	=	45,000
(b) In finished goods	3,000 × 15 × 4	=	1,80,000
(c) In debtors	$\frac{3,000 \times 75 \times 15 \times 8}{100}$	=	2,70,000
			4,95,000
4. Overheads			
(a) In work-in-process	3,000 × 1 × 30	=	90,000
(b) In finished goods	3,000 × 30 × 4	=	3,60,000
(c) In debtors	$\frac{3,000 \times 75 \times 8 \times 30}{100}$	=	5,40,000
			9,90,000

ILLUSTRATION 1.10: From the following information, prepare a statement showing estimated working capital requirement:

(i) Projected annual sales 52,000 units.
(ii) Selling price per unit ₹ 80.
(iii) Analysis of selling price: Material 40%, Labour 30% and Manufacturing expenses 20%.
(iv) Raw materials in stock 4 weeks.
(v) Production process 4 weeks.
(vi) Credit allowed by suppliers 4 weeks.
(vii) Credit allowed to customers 6 weeks.
(viii) Lag in payment of wages 2 weeks.
(ix) Lag in payment of manufacturing expenses one week.
(x) Finished goods inventory 3 weeks.
(xi) Cash in hand is expected to be ₹ 46,000.

Work-in-process involves use of 100% of raw materials and conversion cost equivalent to 50%.

Solution:

Statement Showing Estimated Working Capital Requirement

	₹
A. Current Assets:	
Raw materials	1,28,000
Work-in-process	1,48,000
Finished goods	2,16,000
Debtors	4,80,000
Cash in hand	46,000
	10,18,000
B. Current Liabilities:	
Creditors	1,28,000
Lag in payment of wages	48,000

Lag in payment of manufacturing expenses	16,000
	1,92,000
Working Capital (A–B)	8,26,000

Working Notes:

(i) Raw material cost = 80 × 40% = ₹ 32
Raw material consumption per annum = 52,000 × 32 = ₹ 16,64,000

Raw material inventory = $\frac{16,64,000}{52} \times 4$ = ₹ 1,28,000

(ii) Work-in-process:

Raw material 100% $\frac{16,64,000}{52} \times 4$ = ₹ 1,28,000

Labour 50% $\frac{52,000}{52} \times 24 \times \frac{50}{100}$ = ₹ 12,000

Manufacturing expenses $\frac{52,000}{52} \times 16 \times \frac{50}{100}$ = ₹ 8,000

1,48,000

(iii) Finished goods $\frac{52,000}{52} \times 72 \times 3$ = ₹ 2,16,000

(iv) Debtors $\frac{52,000}{52} \times 80 \times 6$ = ₹ 4,80,000

(v) Creditors $\frac{16,64,000}{52} \times 4$ = ₹ 1,28,000

(vi) Lag in payment of Wages $\frac{52,000}{52} \times 24 \times 2$ = ₹ 48,000

(vii) Lag in payment of manufacturing expenses $\frac{52,000}{52} \times 16 \times 1$
= ₹ 16,000

ILLUSTRATION 1.11: The finance manager of a company is preparing its working capital forecast for the operating capacity at 75%. At present, the company is operating at 50% capacity having production of 24,000 units per year. The following information are gathered by the finance manager:

		₹
Raw material cost per unit		50
Direct labour cost per unit		30
Variable expenses per unit		20
Fixed expenses per unit		10
	Total Cost	110
	Profit	20
	Selling price	130

On 31st March, 2021, the current assets and liabilities were as follows:

Raw material 5,000 units at cost	₹ 25,000
Work-in-process 2,000 units at cost	₹ 16,000
Finished goods 4,000 units at cost	₹ 44,000
Debtors	₹ 2,60,000
Liability for direct labour	₹ 30,000
Liability for expenses	₹ 60,000
Creditors	₹ 1,50,000

The company has decided to operate at 75% capacity from 1st April, 2022 due to increase in demand. The cost and price structure per unit will remain same. The credit allowed to customers, allowed by suppliers, lag in payment of direct labour and expenses will not be changed. Work-in-process may be assumed to be 100% complete as regards materials and 50% as regards direct labour and expenses.

You are required to compute the company's working capital requirement at 75% operating capacity. Further, you are also required to ascertain the additional working capital on account of increase in demand.

Solution:

(i) Monthly production at 75% capacity = $24,000 \times \frac{75}{50} \times \frac{1}{12}$ = 3,000 units

Per annum units at 75% capacity = 3,000 × 12 = 36,000 units

Monthly production at 50% capacity = $\frac{24,000}{12}$ = 2,000 units

(ii) Fixed expenses per month = 2,000 × 10 = ₹ 20,000

(iii) Calculation of time lag:

(a) Raw material 5,000 units = $\frac{5,000}{2,000}$ = 2.5 months

(b) Work-in-process 2,000 units = $\frac{2,000}{2,000}$ = 1 month

(c) Finished goods 4,000 units = $\frac{4,000}{2,000}$ = 2 months

(d) Credit period allowed to debtors:

No. of units = $\frac{2,60,000}{130}$ = 2,000 units

Credit period = $\frac{2,000}{2,000}$ = 1 month

(e) Credit period allowed by suppliers:

No. of units for Creditors = $\frac{1,50,000}{50}$ = 3,000 units

$$\text{Credit period} = \frac{3,000}{2,000} = 1.5 \text{ months}$$

(f) Lag in direct labour payment:

$$\text{No. of units for direct labour} = \frac{30,000}{30} = 1,000 \text{ units}$$

$$\text{Period} = \frac{1,000}{2,000} = \frac{1}{2}\text{month} = 1/2 \text{ month}$$

(g) Lag in expenses payment:

$$\text{No. of units for expenses} = \frac{60,000}{20+10} = 2,000 \text{ units}$$

$$\text{Period} = \frac{2,000}{2,000} = 1 \text{ month}$$

Calculation of Existing Working Capital (31.03.2021)

Working Capital = Current Assets – Current liabilities
= (25,000 + 16,000 + 44,000 + 2,60,000)
– (30,000 + 60,000 + 1,50,000)
= 3,25,000 – 2,40,000
= ₹ 85,000

Statement of Working Capital Requirement at 75% Operating Capacity

			₹
A. Current Assets:			
(i) Stock of raw material	$\frac{36,000 \times 1 \times 2 \times 50}{12}$		3,00,000
(ii) Work-in-process:			
(a) Raw material	$3,000 \times 50 \times \frac{1}{2}$	= 75,000	
(b) Direct labour	$3,000 \times 30 \times \frac{1}{2} \times \frac{50}{100}$	= 22,500	
(c) Variable expenses	$3,000 \times 20 \times \frac{1}{2} \times \frac{50}{100}$	= 15,000	
(d) Fixed expenses	$2,000 \times 10 \times 1 \times \frac{50}{100}$	= 10,000	1,22,500
(iii) Stock of finished goods:			
(a) Raw materials	3,000 × 50 × 2	= 3,00,000	
(b) Direct labour	3,000 × 30 × 2	= 1,80,000	
(c) Variable expenses	3,000 × 20 × 2	= 1,20,000	
(d) Fixed expenses	2,000 × 10 × 2	= 40,000	6,40,000
(iv) Debtors	3,000 × 130 × 1		3,90,000
			14,52,500

B. Current Liabilities:

(i)	Creditors	3,000 × 50 × 1.5	2,25,000
(ii)	Direct labour	3,000 × 30 × 1/2	45,000
(iii)	Variable expenses	3,000 × 20 × 1	60,000
(iv)	Fixed expenses	2,000 × 10 × 1	20,000
			3,50,000

Working Capital (A–B) = 14,52,500 – 3,50,000
= ₹ 11,02,500

Additional Working Capital = 11,02,500 – 85,000
= ₹ 10,17,500

ILLUSTRATION 1.12: A proforma Cost Sheet of Radhika Exports Ltd. provides the following cost data:

Raw material	50%
Wages	20%
Overheads	20%
Profit	10%

The following further particulars are available:

(i) Share Capital ₹ 8,00,000
(ii) 8% Debentures ₹ 2,00,000
(iii) Land and building ₹ 5,00,000
(iv) Plant and machinery ₹ 1,54,000
(v) The level of activity 1,00,000 units
(vi) Selling price ₹ 12 per unit
(vii) Raw materials are expected to remain in store for the period of one month.
(viii) Finished goods are in stock on an average for two months.
(ix) Production in process for one month.
(x) Credit allowed to customers two months.
(xi) Credit allowed by suppliers one month.
(xii) There is regular production and sales cycle.

You are required to prepare:

(a) Statement of Working Capital requirement
(b) Projected Profit and Loss Account and
(c) Projected Balance Sheet

Solution:

(a) Statement of Working Capital Requirement

A. Current Assets	₹
Raw materials	50,000
Work-in-process	90,000
Stock of finished goods	1,80,000
Debtors	1,80,000
	5,00,000

B. Current Liabilities

Creditors	50,000	
	50,000	
Working Capital (A–B) = 5,00,000 – 50,000		₹ 4,50,000

(b) Projected Profit and Loss Account

Particulars	*Amount* (₹)	*Particulars*	*Amount* (₹)
To Raw materials	6,00,000	By Cost of goods sold	10,80,000
To Wages	2,40,000		
To Overheads	2,40,000		
	10,80,000		10,80,000
To Cost of goods sold	10,80,000	By Sales	12,00,000
To Gross profit	1,20,000		
	12,00,000		12,00,000
To Interest on debentures	16,000	By Gross profit	1,20,000
To Net profit	1,04,000		
	1,20,000		1,20,000

Projected Balance Sheet

Liabilities	*Amount* (₹)	*Assets*	*Amount* (₹)
Share Capital	8,00,000	Land and Building	5,00,000
Net Profit	1,04,000	Plant and Machinery	1,54,000
8% Debentures	2,00,000	Raw Materials	50,000
Creditors	50,000	Work-in-process	90,000
		Finished Goods	1,80,000
		Debtors	1,80,000
	11,54,000		11,54,000

Working Notes:

(i) Stock of Raw materials $1{,}00{,}000 \times 12 \times \frac{1}{12} \times \frac{50}{100}$ = ₹ 50,000

(ii) Stock of Finished goods $1{,}00{,}000 \times 12 \times \frac{2}{12} \times \frac{90}{100}$ = ₹ 1,80,000

(iii) Work-in-process

(a) Raw materials $1{,}00{,}000 \times 6 \times \frac{1}{12}$ = ₹ 50,000

(b) Wages $1{,}00{,}000 \times 12 \times \frac{1}{12} \times \frac{20}{100}$ = ₹ 20,000

(c) Overheads $1{,}00{,}000 \times 12 \times \frac{1}{12} \times \frac{20}{100}$ = ₹ 20,000 ₹ 90,000

(iv) Debtors $1,00,000 \times 12 \times \frac{2}{12} \times \frac{90}{100}$ = ₹ 1,80,000

(v) Creditors $1,00,000 \times 12 \times \frac{1}{12} \times \frac{50}{100}$ = ₹ 50,000

THEORETICAL QUESTIONS

I. Short Answer Type Questions

1. Define Working Capital.
2. Explain Net Working Capital.
3. Distinguish between Gross and Net Working Capital.
4. Define Fixed Working Capital.
5. Explain Seasonal and Special Working Capital.
6. What is Operating Cycle concept of Working Capital?
7. Define Net Operating Cycle.
8. Explain the nature of working capital.
9. Explain two factors affecting the working capital need.
10. Explain the Regression Analysis Technique of estimating working capital need.

II. Long Answer Type Questions

1. Define working capital. Explain the features and objectives of working capital.
2. What are the various kinds of working capital? Explain.
3. Explain and illustrate the operating cycle concept of working capital. How this concept is useful in taking decision regarding working capital in a manufacturing organisation? Describe.
4. Explain the nature and need of working capital.
5. Explain the factors influencing working capital requirements and discuss their importance.
6. What are the techniques of estimating working capital need? Explain the method of estimating different components of working capital with illustration.
7. Explain the operating cycle method of estimating working capital need.
8. Write notes on:
   (i) Gross and Net Working Capital
   (ii) Fixed and Variable Working Capital
   (iii) Need for Working Capital

III. Numerical Questions

1. Bharat Industries Ltd. is going to start its business on 1st January, 2022. The following information are made available:

	₹
Stock of finished goods	10,000
Stock of stores and materials	13,000
Credit allowed to customers:	
Inland sales (4 weeks)	2,08,000
Export sales (2 weeks)	1,04,000
Payment in advance (half yearly basis)	32,000
Lag in payments:	
Wages (2 weeks)	1,56,000
Rent (4 weeks)	52,000
Salary to staff (4 weeks)	1,04,000
Miscellaneous expenses (4 weeks)	26,000
Salary to manager (4 weeks)	91,000
Purchase of materials (4 weeks)	52,000

You are required to estimate average amount of working capital which will be required in first year of working by adding 10% for contingencies.

Ans: Working Capital ₹ 30,800

2. A proforma Cost sheet of Glob Manufacturing Company Ltd. provides the following particulars:

	₹
Materials per unit	75
Direct labour per unit	35
Overheads per unit	65
Total Cost per unit	175
Profit per unit	25
Selling price per unit	200

The following further particulars are available:

(i) Raw materials are in stock on an average for one month.
(ii) Raw materials are in process on an average for half month.
(iii) Finished goods are in stock on an average for one month.
(iv) Credit allowed by suppliers is one month.
(v) Lag in payment of wages is half month.
(vi) Lag in payment of overheads is one month.
(vii) One fourth output is sold against cash.
(viii) Cash in hand and at Bank is expected to be ₹ 30,000.
(ix) Credit allowed to customers is two months.

You are required to prepare a statement showing the working capital need to finance the level of activity of 1,04,000 units of production.

You may assume that production is carried on evenly throughout the year, wages and overheads accrue similarly and a time period of four weeks is equivalent to a month.

Ans: Working Capital ₹ 36,70,000 **(MFC B.H.U.)**

3. The Balance Sheet of Solar Energy Ltd. as on 31st December, 2021 is as follows:

Balance Sheet of Solar Energy Ltd. as on 31st December, 2021

Liabilities	*Amount (₹)*	*Assets*	*Amount (₹)*
Share Capital	3,20,000	Goodwill	15,000
General Reserve	50,000	Land and Building	50,000
7% Debentures	40,000	Plant and Machinery	85,000
Profit and Loss Account	50,000	Stock	1,50,000
Creditors	60,000	Debtors	80,000
Bills Payable	20,000	Cash	60,000
Outstanding Expenses	20,000	Bank	1,20,000
	5,60,000		5,60,000

The company's turnover for the year 2021 was ₹ 20 lakh. It anticipates sales ₹ 50 lakh in 2022. Estimate working capital requirement on the basis of percentage of sales method.

Ans: Working Capital ₹ 7,75,000

4. Index Garment Company Ltd. is a famous manufacturer and exporter of garments. The sales and current assets of the company for the period of five years are as follows:

Year	*Sales (₹ in lakh)*	*Current Assets (₹ in lakh)*
2018	32	22
2019	44	27
2020	52	31
2021	57	43
2022	69	45

Estimate working capital requirement for the year 2023 according to Regression Analysis Method. Anticipated sales are ₹ 87 lakh.

Ans: Working Capital ₹ 58.32 lakh

5. Suvardhanam Ltd., a manufacturing firm, has applied for working capital finance from a commercial bank. You are requested by the bank to prepare an estimate of working capital requirement of the company. You may add 10% to your estimated figure to account for contingencies. A proforma cost sheet of the company provides the following information:

		Cost per unit ₹
Raw materials		55
Direct labour		20
Overheads		40
	Total Cost	115
	Profit	25
	Selling Price	140

Additional information:

(i) Raw materials are in stock on an average for one month.
(ii) Raw materials are in process half a month.
(iii) Finished goods are in stock on an average for one month.
(iv) Credit allowed by suppliers is one month.
(v) Lag in payment of wages is one week.
(vi) Lag in payment of overheads is one month.
(vii) 25% output is sold against cash.
(viii) Cash in hand is estimated to be ₹ 50,000
(ix) Credit allowed to customers is two months.
(x) Production is 1,04,000 units.

You may assume that production is carried out evenly throughout the year. A time period of 4 weeks is equivalent to one month.

Ans: Working Capital ₹ 26,95,000 **(M.B.A. FM B.H.U.)**

6. The following information are provided by the DVP Ltd. for the year ending 31st March, 2015:

Raw material storage period	50 days
Work-in-process conversion period	18 days
Finished goods storage period	22 days
Debt collection period	45 days
Creditors' payment period	55 days
Annual operating cost	₹ 21 lakh
(including depreciation of ₹ 2,10,000)	
(1 year = 360 days)	

You are required to calculate:

(i) Operating cycle period.
(ii) Number of operating cycles in a year.
(iii) Amount of working capital required for the company on cash cost basis.
(iv) The company is a market leader in its product, there is virtually no competitor in the market. Based on market research, it is planning to discontinue sales on credit and deliver products based on pre-payment. There by it can reduce its working capital requirement substantially. What would be the reduction in working capital requirement due to such decision.

(C.A. Inter)

Ans: (i) Operating cycle period 80 days, (ii) No. of operating cycle in a year 4.5, (iii) Working capital ₹ 4,20,000, and (iv) Reduction in working capital ₹ 2,36,250.

7. M N Ltd. is commencing a new project for manufacture of electric toys. The following cost information has been ascertained for annual production of 60,000 units at full capacity:

		Amount per unit ₹
Raw materials		20
Direct labour		15
Manufacturing overheads:		
Variable	15	
Fixed	10	25
Selling and Distribution overheads:		
Variable	3	
Fixed	1	4
	Total Cost	64
	Profit	16
	Selling Price	80

In the first year of operations expected production and sales are 40,000 units and 35,000 units respectively. To assess the need of working capital, the following additional information is available:

(i) Stock of raw materials 3 months consumption
(ii) Credit allowed for Debtors 1.5 months
(iii) Credit allowed by creditors 4 months
(iv) Lag in payment of wages 1 month
(v) Lag in payment of overheads 1/2 month
(vi) Cash in hand and at Bank is expected to be ₹ 60,000
(vii) Provision for contingencies is required @ 10% of working capital requirement including that provision.

You are required to prepare projected statement of working capital requirement of its first year of operations. Debtors are taken at cost. **(C.A. Inter)**

Ans: Working capital ₹ 4,99,769

8. A proforma cost sheet of a company provides the following data:

		₹
Raw material cost per unit		117
Direct labour cost per unit		49
Factory overheads cost per unit (includes depreciation of ₹ 18 per unit at budgeted level of activity)		98
	Total cost per unit	264
	Profit	36
	Selling price per unit	300

Following additional information is available:

Average raw material in stock	4 weeks
Average work-in-process stock (% completion with respect to materials 80% labour and overheads 60%)	2 weeks

Finished goods in stock	3 weeks
Credit period allowed to debtors	6 weeks
Credit period availed from suppliers	8 weeks
Time lag in payment of wages	1 week
Time lag in payment of overheads	2 weeks

The company sells one-fifth of the output against cash and maintains cash balance of ₹ 2,50,000.

Required:

Prepare a statement showing estimate of working capital needed to finance a budgeted activity level of 78,000 units of production. You may assume that production is carried on evenly throughout the year and wages and overheads accrue similarly. **(C.A. Inter)**

Ans: Working Capital ₹ 26,25,700.

9. Looks and Care Ltd. proposes to manufacture a cosmetic product which has been developed by its research and development department. The following information is available:

(i) Cost structure:

Raw materials per unit	₹ 30
Wages per unit	₹ 10
Overheads per unit	₹ 5

(ii) Level of activity 52,000 units

(iii) Selling price per unit ₹ 50

(iv) Budgeted stock levels:

Raw materials 3 weeks

Work-in-progress 1 week (material 100%, wages and overheads 50%).

Finished goods 2 weeks

(v) Debtors are allowed credit 4 weeks

(vi) Creditors are allowed credit 4 weeks

(vii) Lag in payment of wages 2 weeks

(viii) Lag in payment of overheads 2 weeks

(ix) Cash in hand required ₹ 50,000.

Additional information:

	₹
Share Capital	10,00,000
6% Debentures	3,00,000
Land and Building	7,00,000
Plant and Machinery	4,00,000
Furniture	1,37,000

You are required to prepare:

(a) Statement of Working Capital Requirement

(b) Forecast Profit and Loss Account

(c) Forecast Balance Sheet

Ans: (a) Working Capital ₹ 3,05,000, (b) Net Profit ₹ 2,42,000, and (c) Balance Sheet Total ₹ 16,92,000.

2

Working Capital–II

CHAPTER OVERVIEW AND LEARNING OBJECTIVES

Financing of working capital depends upon the type of working capital, i.e., fixed and temporary working capital. The common belief is that temporary working capital should be financed from short-term sources while fixed working capital should be financed from long-term sources. There are different sources for financing long-term working capital, i.e., share capital, debentures, long-term loans, etc. The short-term working capital may be obtained from trade credit, accrual accounts, cash credit, overdraft, etc. Thus, financing of working capital is the mix of long-term and short-term sources. The proportion of finance mix depends upon the number of factors like seasonal, liquidity, cost of finance, etc. There are different approaches to determine working capital finance mix. In order to judge the efficient utilisation of working capital, working capital ratios are used. The working capital should neither be excess nor inadequate because both have their pros and cons. Therefore, symptoms of poor working capital should be identified from time-to-time.

Learning Objectives: *The students will be able to:*

- Explain the concept of working capital financing
- Understand the long- and short-term sources of financing working capital
- Implement strategies for working capital financing mix
- Calculate working capital ratios
- List adequacy and inadequacy of working capital
- Know the dangers of excessive working capital
- Identify the symptoms of poor working capital management

2.1 INTRODUCTION

We have learned that there are two types of working capital, i.e., fixed working capital and temporary working capital. The amount locked up in different components of current assets which are to be maintained during the lifetime of the business is permanent working capital. This is to be maintained as per the need of the business because they do not generate any return. This is the reason why current ratio has to be substantially above one. A good current ratio is in favour of creditors and shows the creditworthiness of the firm. Tandon Committee has referred fixed working capital as "core current assets." Thus, in such situation the permanent working capital must be secured by permanent sources, i.e., long-term funds. The cost of such financing is relatively cheaper. On the other hand, temporary working capital is used for carrying day-to-day operations and meeting any exigencies. This is required for purchasing of raw materials, payment of wages and salaries, maintenance of cash balance, etc. The common belief is that temporary working capital should be financed from short-term sources, i.e., bank credits. A word of caution is necessary because the cost of such financing is costlier. Supplier of such working capital may withdraw the facility on short notice. There are no specific guidelines as to how finance the working capital needs. It all depends upon the attitude of finance manager, i.e., aggressive or conservative, nature and situation of business. In manufacturing organisation the pattern of the financing may be different to service organisation.

2.2 FINANCING OF WORKING CAPITAL

In exercising the choice of securing finance, cost of credit, dependability on the source of credit and flexibility in selection of sources should be given due weightage. The financing of working capital may be classified as financing of long-term working capital and financing of short-term working capital.

2.2.1 Financing of Long-term Working Capital

The firm has to maintain a definite volume of current assets, i.e., stock, debtors and cash in the business to carry-out its daily operations smoothly. The amount invested in such current assets is more or less blocked during the life of the business though these assets changed from one form to another in the process of circulation. Therefore, long-term or fixed working capital should be financed through long-term sources. The purpose is that the cost of such funds is less in comparison to short-term sources. The long-term sources have less risk and increases the liquidity of the firm since the firm is not supposed to repay loans regularly at frequent intervals. The following sources may be used for financing long-term working capital needs:

1. **Share Capital:** Share capital consists of equity shares and preference shares. Generally, equity shares are issued by the company for obtaining the funds. It is one of the important sources of raising funds for long-term capital. Equity share capital represents the ownership interest. Equity shares are variable income securities and does not create any fixed burden on the profits of the company in the form of dividend. Preference shares are hybrid security containing features of

fixed income securities and the share ownership. Therefore, funds are raised through equity shares for financing the fixed working capital requirements.

2. **Debentures:** Debentures are another source of raising long-term finance. This is a debt capital or fixed income bearing security. The holders of debentures are creditors of the company. A fixed rate of interest is paid at fixed intervals every year irrespective of the earnings of the company. Therefore, it creates a fixed burden on the company. On the other hand, the company may also enjoy benefits of trading on equity, tax benefits, etc. by issuing debentures. Therefore, a progressive company having sound liquid position may use this source for raising funds for financing permanent working capital needs.
3. **Bonds:** This is also fixed income bearing security and similar to the debentures. Bond is a long-term debt instrument that promises to pay fixed annual amount as interest for a specified period of time. The interest rate on the bond may be fixed or floating. The redemption date and redemption value are stated in the bond certificate at the time of issue. This type of source for raising the fund for permanent working capital need may be used by the company having future development projects.
4. **Retained Earnings:** Generally, the company does not declare whole earnings in the form of dividend to shareholders but a certain part of it is retained in the business to meet the growing needs of the business. The part of earnings which is retained in the business is called retained earnings. This is an economical source of financing to meet the working capital needs. It acts as support to the company in handling the adverse situations such as shocks of trade cycle, market uncertainty, etc. It also helps in the sound liquidity position of the company. This source may be used by the company during any exigency or future growth of the business.
5. **Public Deposits:** The companies are also using public deposits to finance their working capital needs. These deposits are unsecured, risky, having no tax benefits, etc. The company generally offers higher rate of interest as compared to bank interest rate. Therefore, the public deposits have shown growth in the amount as well as in number of companies offering public deposits. The cost of funds raised through public deposits is less than the interest rate charged by financial institutions. Public deposits are subject to the government regulations. Public deposits are not definite source of financing working capital as and when need arises because before offering public deposits, the company has to complete certain formalities for issue.
6. **Long-term Loans from Financial Institutions:** The companies can also meet their permanent working capital requirements by raising long-term funds from banks and other financial institutions in addition

to share capital, debenture, bonds, public deposits, etc. It is negotiated source of financing by signing an agreement between borrower and lending institution. The major plus point of this source is that the repayment shall be made after stipulated period or in instalments in a number of years. Therefore, by earning the income the payment shall be made. The firm can also enjoy tax benefit on the amount of interest paid. Progressive firms or having developmental projects may use this source of finance by comparing other sources of financing permanent working capital.

2.2.2 Financing of Short-term Working Capital

Financing of short-term working capital needs is a regular feature of the firm. Short-term sources are used to meet the day-to-day requirements or in exigent circumstances. The duration of such funds does not exceed more than a year. Short-term sources of raising funds may be spontaneous or negotiated sources. Spontaneous sources arise naturally in the course of business like, creditors, B/P, etc. Similarly, financing which has to be negotiated with lending institutions is called negotiated finance like cash credit, overdraft, etc. The short-term working capital may be obtained from the following sources:

1. Trade Credit: Trade credit is one of the important sources of short-term working capital. It is a facility provided by the vendor/suppliers to business firms by deferring the payment to a definite future. In other words, when goods are purchased by the business firm on credit from the seller firm obtained the working capital up-to the amount of purchase and the period till it is repaid. Therefore, it is said as spontaneous source of finance for short-term, i.e., in-days or few months. This source does not include retail or consumer credit. It is more useful for small and medium firms.

Characteristics of Trade Credit

The following are important features of trade credit:

(i) Trade credit is a spontaneous source of finance for short-term.
(ii) It is normally extended to all types of business firms having good creditworthiness.
(iii) The availability of credit depends upon the relationship of buyer and seller and repayment reputation.
(iv) The trade credit bears negligible cost.
(v) The business firms are heavily dependent on this source of finance.
(vi) It is different from instalment credit.
(vii) It does not require any security margin.

Types of Trade Credit

Trade credit may be in the form of:

(i) Open account trade credit where buyer does not require to sign any agreement or instrument. Such credit is termed as creditors.

(ii) Trade credit may be in the form of acceptance credit arrangement where the buyer signs an agreement or legal evidence, i.e., acceptance of a bill of exchange or gives a promissory note. It is termed as bills payable.

Terms of Trade Credit

The terms of trade credit are decided by the vendor or supplier of the goods. The size of the credit and credit period will be decided by the supplier taking into account creditworthiness (new firm) and past performance of the existing firm in terms of payment of dues in time, relationship with the buyer, volume of business, etc. Sometimes supplier also allows cash discount to motivate buyers for early payment of dues. The credit period may start either from the date of despatch of goods or from the date of goods received. Generally, it starts from the date of receipt of the goods.

Merits of Trade Credit

The following are the merits of trade credit:

(i) It is easily available.

(ii) It is available on regular basis subject to relationship and creditworthiness.

(iii) It is available without any security.

(iv) It is flexible with increase or decrease in the size of business.

(v) It is interest-free source of finance.

Demerits of Trade Credit

The following may be the demerits of trade credit:

(i) There may be chances of loss of cash discount due to purchase on credit.

(ii) In appearance, there is no explicit cost of trade credit but it may have some implicit cost to cover operational expenses, i.e., maintenance of accounts, collection charges, bad debts, etc.

(iii) The buyer has to forego price concessions available on cash purchases by negotiation.

(iv) The amount and period of credit will be as per the attitude of the supplier.

(v) The period of trade credit, i.e., long or short may affect the cost of credit.

2. Accrual Accounts: Accrual accounts are spontaneous source of finance. These are expenses which have been incurred but paid later. The accrual accounts may include wages and salaries paid monthly, fortnightly or weekly basis, interest accrued on loans, utility bills, taxes, etc. Thus, longer the period of payment, the more availability of funds for meeting the short-term working capital needs. The main advantage of this source of finance is that it is costless and interest free. As far as the demerit of such source of finance is that the firm cannot stretch accrual accounts for long period after due date.

3. Commercial Paper: The commercial paper (CP) is introduced in Indian financial market on the recommendations of the Vaghul Committee. The Reserve Bank of India has issued guidelines within that framework CPs can be issued. These guidelines are modified by the RBI from time to time. A company may issue commercial paper for raising debt fund to meet the short-term requirement of working capital. Commercial paper is a form of usance promissory note, negotiable, unsecured with a fixed maturity period. It can be issued directly to the investor or through the dealers (bank/merchant bankers). When the CPs are directly issued by the company to the investors without the involvement of dealer, the CP is called direct paper and if issued through dealers, it is called dealer paper. As per the SEBI guidelines, the company must have minimum credit rating A-3. A commercial paper can be issued for maturities between a minimum of seven days and not more than a year from the date of issue. A Commercial paper can be issued either in the form of promissory note or in dematerialised form. CP can be issued in multiples of ₹ 5 lakh. CPs are issued at discount and redeemed at their face value. A company is eligible to issue Commercial paper if:

(a) The tangible net-worth is not less than ₹ 4 crore as per the latest audited balance sheet;
(b) The working capital limit of the company has been sanctioned by the banks or financial institutions; and
(c) The borrower's account should be classified as standard.

Commercial papers are flexible in terms of maturities. The company can buyback CPs on approval of the Board of Directors. It is unsecured and does not create any lien on the assets of the company. CPs are highly liquid as they are negotiable instruments. The merit of the CP is the reduced rate of interest as compared to that charged by the commercial banks/financial institutions. The main demerit is that this type of source of fund can generally be used by those companies having good credit rating and good financial track record continuously for example blue chip companies. The other demerit is that the issuance of CP is subjected to regulatory control and the procedure of issue is also lengthy.

4. Factoring: This is another one of the recent sources of financing the working capital requirements. Factoring is a financial service covering financing and taking the responsibility of collection of book debts in domestic as well as international trade. Factoring is an arrangement between factor (intermediary) and client (business firm) which have legal relationship. The factoring organisations are professionally engaged. For rendering this service, the discount or fee is charged by the factor. In other words, it is a method of financing against the book debts of a client. Often factor may provide financial assistance to the client by advancing 80% to 90% of the amount of book debts and the balance is paid after the maturity of the document. It is a continuous arrangement between the factor and the client. Factoring may be non-recourse and recourse both. In case of non-recourse factoring, factor assumes 100% credit risks which means in case if the debtors fail to repay the debts, the entire risk is born by the factor while in recourse factoring factor does not assume 100% credit risk which means the client is not protected against the risk of bad debts. Financing of the book debts improves the liquidity of the client. Apart from financing service, factoring institutions also advise the client regarding the selection of potential trade debtors to minimise the risk of bad debts. The basic demerit of factoring is that it is an expensive source of short-term credit.

5. Working Capital Finance by Banks: Commercial banks are the only recognised sources of short-term working capital finance to the industry. The major part of the working capital is provided by the banks because every firm has a bank account and maintains good relation with the bank. The banks are helping to the industry by extending credit in different forms on regular basis as well as in exigent circumstances. The main categories of credit facilities provided by the banks are:

(i) **Cash Credit:** Cash credit facility is provided by the banks to its client for meeting their short-term financial requirements. It is an arrangement between the bank and the customer by which bank allows to the customer to borrow money up-to pre-fixed period as and when need arises. Cash credit facility is provided on the basis of some tangible securities or guarantees. The securities offered by the customer are in the nature of hypothecation of stock. A borrower can withdraw money many times in a day up-to the pre-fixed limit. The borrower can also deposit surplus, if any, in the account. The interest on cash credit account is calculated on a daily product basis and not on the entire amount sanctioned. The advantage of this type of credit is that the borrower need not to borrow the whole of the amount of limit fixed.

(ii) **Loans:** Banks also provides short-term loans to the firm. The loans are given in lump sum against the security. A definite sum is sanctioned under the loan by the bank to the borrower. The interest is charged on the whole amount sanctioned by the bank from the date of sanction. The repayment of the loan amount may be made either in lump sum at the closing date or in instalment from time to time during the period of the loan. The loan facility may be used by the firm to meet seasonal requirement of working capital, e.g., purchase of raw materials in season to avail the benefit of price decline or in exigencies other than day-to-day need.

(iii) **Overdraft:** Overdraft facility is available on current account in bank. It is a short-term arrangement between the bank and current account holder. The holder of the account is allowed to withdraw the money more than the balance to its credit up-to a limit agreed upon. The interest is charged on daily withdrawn amount. The holder may repay that amount any time. Overdraft account may be fully secured, partly secured or unsecured. Generally, unsecured facility is available to customers on the basis of relationship with the bank. Overdraft facility is very flexible. The cost of finance is also economical.

(iv) **Bills Discounting Facility:** Bank also provides finance to the firm against the bills raised. In other words, the bank provides finance for a short period till the acceptor of the bill makes the payment. Bills discounting means the bank purchases the bill and credit the discounted amount in customer account. The rate of discount is decided by the bank. Bank presents the bill to the acceptor of bill for collection on due date. In case the acceptor does not pay the amount on due date, the bank debit the client account with full amount of the bill along with penal interest/expenses. Therefore, the bank may be selective in discounting the bill. This facility is available without any collateral security.

2.3 STRATEGIES FOR WORKING CAPITAL FINANCING MIX

The objective of working capital management is to maximise the value of the firm. The financing of working capital need is to decide the mix of long-term and short-term sources. In other words, what source of finance should be used for financing of fixed and variable working capital. The proportion of finance mix for current assets depends upon the number of factors like seasonal and cyclical factors, liquidity, cost of finance, financial flexibility, etc. Apart from these factors, the working capital mix also depends upon the attitude of the management and finance manager whether they want to take risk or play safe. Generally, there are three approaches for determining the working capital financing mix.

2.3.1 Conservative Approach

Under this approach, the attitude of the finance manager is to play safe. The finance manager does not want to take high risk which means the entire investment in current assets (permanent and variable) should be finance from long-term sources. In this strategy, the management keeps the permanent current assets more than the requirement with the objective that any sudden change in the demand of the market and production schedule could be met easily. But low-risk taking approach will result into low profit. This approach assures the continuous flow of fund for working capital need as and when arises and smooth operational working. Sometimes, long-term financing covers more than the total requirement of working capital. Under such situation, the finance manager takes the steps to invest excess amount in short-term securities. But it does not mean that short-term sources will not be used. These sources may be used in case of any exigency and for meeting any seasonal requirement.

Features

The distinct features are:

- (i) To maintain good liquidity position of the firm.
- (ii) To ensure the availability of funds for working capital need all the time.
- (iii) To minimise the risk of shortage of funds.
- (iv) High cost of financing on account of interest and carrying cost of finished goods.
- (v) The tenet of low-risk–low-profit will apply.
- (vi) The excess fund will remain idle in the business due to delay in investing in short-term marketable securities.

The conservative financing approach is depicted in Figure 2.1:

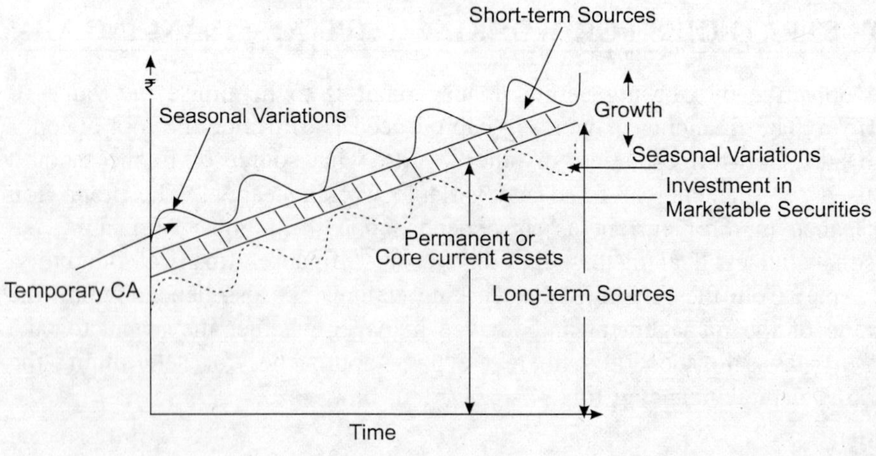

FIGURE 2.1 Conservative financing approach for determining the working capital financing mix.

The above figure shows that the permanent and temporary current assets both except seasonal variations in temporary current assets will be financed by long-term sources. The shaded portion represents the part of temporary current assets. The seasonal variations in temporary current assets will be finance by short-term sources. Similarly, any variation in permanent current assets generating surplus will be invested in marketable securities.

2.3.2 Aggressive Approach

Aggressive approach represents the risk-taking attitude of the finance manager. Current assets are monitored just to meet the current liabilities and no extra provision of current assets are made. It shows that the current ratio will always be less than the standard norm of 2:1. Thus, this approach minimises the investment in current assets resulting into low cost of financing. Under this approach, the permanent or core current assets which are required to be maintained all the time in the business will be financed by long-term sources and any seasonal variations and day-to-day requirements will be financed by short-term sources. It means the use of short-term sources will be on regular and frequent basis resulting into higher cost of finance. In such situation, the finance manager should be conscious all the time for arranging funds for working capital requirement. For the success of this approach, it is essential that the finance manager has to maintain good relations with banks and other financial institutions so that in short notice funds could be made available to the firm. The drawback of this approach is that any sudden change in market demand and production schedule cannot be met in short period since no cushion of current assets is maintained. High risk-taking approach will result into high profit but the cost of short-term sources is always higher than the long-term sources of financing. The aggressive approach is depicted in Figure 2.2

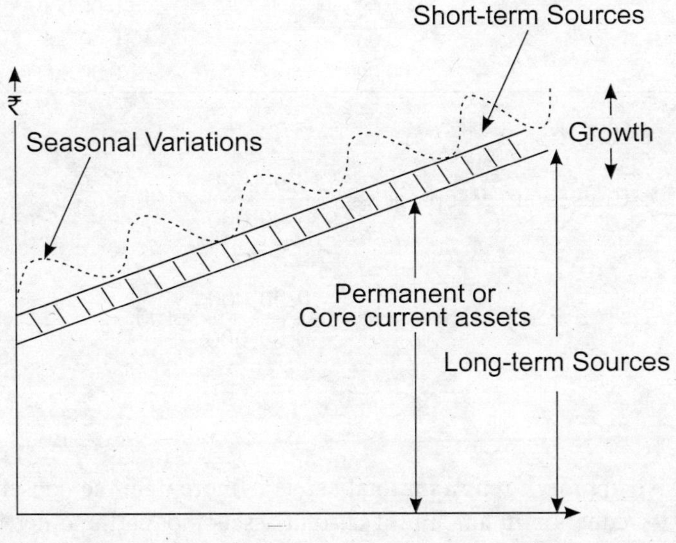

FIGURE 2.2 Aggressive approach for determining the working capital financing mix.

The above figure shows that the permanent or core current assets will be financed by long-term sources. The shaded portion of the figure reflects the variation in permanent current assets. The seasonal variations, if any, will be financed by short-term sources.

Example 2.1:

The following information are available of the XY Company Ltd.:

Particulars	*Conservative approach* (₹)	*Aggressive approach* (₹)
Sales	50,00,000	50,00,000
Fixed assets	20,00,000	20,00,000
Current assets	15,00,000	10,00,000
EBIT	30%	30%
Interest on debt	2,00,000	2,00,000
Tax	3,00,000	3,00,000

You are required to calculate return on investment and comment on for adopting conservative and aggressive approach.

Solution:

Particulars	*Conservative approach* (₹)	*Aggressive approach* (₹)
Sales	**50,00,000**	**50,00,000**
EBIT 30%	15,00,000	15,00,000
Less: Interest on debt	2,00,000	2,00,000
EBT	13,00,000	13,00,000
Less: Tax	3,00,000	3,00,000
EAT	10,00,000	10,00,000
Total investment:		
Fixed assets	20,00,000	20,00,000
Current assets	15,00,000	10,00,000
Total	35,00,000	30,00,000

Return on Investment:

$$\text{Conservative approach} = \frac{10,00,000}{35,00,000} \times 100$$

$$= 28.57\%$$

$$\text{Aggressive approach} = \frac{10,00,000}{30,00,000} \times 100$$

$$= 33.33\%$$

Comment

Under aggressive approach return on total assets is more than the conservative approach due to reduction in amount of current assets though the other factors are same. This confirms the policy of high risk and high return and vice-versa.

2.3.3 Hedging Approach

Under hedging approach, financing of working capital is done in such a way that the maturity of the debt should match with the maturity of working capital financing need. Therefore, it is also said as matching approach. In this approach, it is suggested that the permanent working capital need should be financed by long-term sources because permanent working capital does not vary overtime. The temporary or seasonal working capital which fluctuates from time to time should be financed by short-term sources as per need. The basic drawback of this approach is that the temporary or seasonal working capital requirement cannot be ascertained in advance due to fluctuating nature. Therefore, the process of matching maturities of debt with the maturity of short-term working capital need cannot be done accurately. There are chances that the maturity of debt may fall before or after the working capital need.

Trade-off between Hedging and Conservative Approach

The level of trade-off between hedging and conservative approaches largely depends upon the attitude of the management and finance manager who are responsible for taking decision towards the perception of risk. Conservative approach shows the low-risk perception while hedging approach reflects high risk perception. The level of trade-off may also differ according to requirement of working capital, i.e., short-term or long-term need. Thus, in determining the level of trade-off between these approaches may be a mid-path, i.e., average requirement of working capital. The average may be calculated by taking into account the maximum working capital requirement and minimum working capital requirement over the time. Thus, it may be suggested that average working capital need should be financed by long-term sources and if any seasonal variations are above the average working capital need may be financed by short-term sources. The main difficulty is that the estimation of maximum and minimum working capital requirements cannot be judged perfectly.

2.4 WORKING CAPITAL RATIO

It is the objective of every firm that working capital must be always in circulation and generate surplus for the business. It should neither be in excess nor in short. Therefore, the firm should maintain a sound working position or liquidity in the business. In order to judge the efficient utilisation of working capital, ratio analysis technique is used. For the purpose, certain ratios are used which may be:

2.4.1 Current Ratio

Current ratio is the tool of measuring the ability of the firm to meet its short-term commitments in time and carry out its day-to-day operations smoothly. In other words, it is a tool of measuring short-term stability of the firm. The ratio is a relationship between current assets and current liabilities. It is widely used to make the analysis of short-term liquidity of the firm. It can be expressed as:

$$\text{Current Ratio} = \frac{\text{Current Assets}}{\text{Current Liabilities}}$$

Interpretation

It is generally accepted that ideal standard ratio is 2:1 which means current assets should be two times of current liabilities. The purpose is that the current obligations should be met as and when they arise. Thus, the layman's interpretation is that the higher current ratio indicates firm is liquid or having sound liquid position and vice-versa. But it should not be followed blindly by the finance manager. There may be many causes of higher or low current ratio. Higher current ratio may not be favourable due to the following reasons:

- Turnover of stock is slow due to poor sales.
- Debtors are overdue due to unsatisfactory collection efforts.
- Idleness of cash and bank balances.
- Decline in value of current assets.

Similarly, low current ratio may be due to the following reasons:

- Non-availability of sufficient funds to pay off liabilities.
- Resources may not warrant activities.

The current ratio does not take into account the quality of current assets. Therefore, it may be said that too much reliance on the ratio is not good for the firm and further analysis is required.

2.4.2 Quick Ratio

The quick ratio is the more rigorous test of liquidity. It implicates the ability of the firm to pay its current liabilities in short period or as and when due. The ratio establishes the relationship between liquid assets and current liabilities. Liquid assets are those assets which can be converted or realised in cash without sacrificing the value in short period or immediately. Cash is the most liquid assets. The quick ratio is also called liquid ratio and acid test ratio. The ratio may be expressed as follows:

$$\text{Quick Ratio} = \frac{\text{Liquid Assets}}{\text{Current Liabilities}}$$

Liquid Assets = Current Assets – (Inventories + Prepaid Expenses)

Interpretation

Generally quick ratio of 1:1 is considered standard. The 1:1 means for every rupee of current liabilities one rupee of liquid assets is available for payment. Therefore, it is a better test of short-term solvency of the firm. The liquid ratio represents that the firm is liquid and vice-versa. But high ratio all the time is not in favour of the firm because there is no guarantee that the debtors will be realised in time with full due amount. On the contrary, low value of quick ratio may be in favour of the firm if the firm is able to convert inventories into sales quickly.

2.4.3 Absolute Liquid Ratio

The absolute liquid ratio is also known as cash ratio or super quick ratio. The ratio establishes the relationship between absolute liquid assets and current liabilities. The acceptable norm for this ratio is 1:2, i.e., 50%. It is considered that rupee one of absolute liquid assets is sufficient for meeting the current liabilities of rupees two. The reason is that all the creditors will not be due at the same time and in the mean-time cash may be realised from debtors and inventory conversion into sales. However, this ratio has importance for financial institutions to meet the cash demand immediately. The trading and manufacturing organisations have some cushion for making payments to the creditors. Therefore, the ratio may not be important for such organisations. Moreover, short-term cash requirement can be judged or forecasted on the basis of properly drawn cash budget. The ratio may be expressed as follows:

$$\text{Absolute Liquid Ratio} = \frac{\text{Absolute Liquid Assets}}{\text{Current Liabilities}}$$

Absolute Liquid Assets = Cash and Bank Balances + Short-term Marketable Securities or Investments

ILLUSTRATION 2.1: The Balance Sheet of XY Company Ltd. as at 31st March, 2021 is as follows:

Liabilities	*Amount* (₹)	*Assets*	*Amount* (₹)
Share Capital	15,00,000	Goodwill	1,00,000
7% Debentures	2,80,000	Land and Building	8,00,000
Long-term Loan	1,20,000	Plant and Machinery	6,00,000
Trade Payable	1,00,000	Furniture	1,05,000
Bills Payable	20,000	Trade Investments	1,50,000
Bank Overdraft	25,000	Marketable Securities	40,000
Rent Payable	20,000	Sundry Debtors	2,00,000
Dividend Payable	20,000	Stock	1,00,000
Provision for Tax	25,000	Cash and Bank	30,000
Prov. for Doubtful Debts	20,000	Prepaid Expenses	5,000
	21,30,000		21,30,000

Calculate the following ratios and comment upon the short-term financial position of the company:

(a) Current Ratio
(b) Quick Ratio
(c) Cash Ratio

Solution:

(a) $\text{Current Ratio} = \dfrac{\text{Current Assets}}{\text{Current Liabilities}}$

Current Assets = 40,000 + (2,00,000 – 20,000) + 1,00,000 + 30,000 + 5,000
= ₹ 3,55,000

Current Liabilities = 1,00,000 + 20,000 + 25,000 + 20,000 + 20,000 + 25,000
= ₹ 2,10,000

$\text{Current Ratio} = \dfrac{3,55,000}{2,10,000} = 1.69:1$

(b) $\text{Quick Ratio} = \dfrac{\text{Liquid Assets}}{\text{Current Liabilities}}$

Liquid Assets = Current Assets – (Stock + Prepaid Expenses)
= ₹ 3,55,000 – (1,00,000 + 5,000)
= ₹ 2,50,000

$\text{Quick Ratio} = \dfrac{2,50,000}{2,10,000} = 1.19:1$

(c) $\text{Cash Ratio} = \dfrac{\text{Absolute Liquid Assets}}{\text{Current Liabilities}}$

Absolute Liquid Assets = 40,000 + 30,000 = ₹ 70,000

$\text{Cash Ratio} = \dfrac{70,000}{2,10,000} = 0.33:1$

Comments

Current ratio (1.69:1) of the company is below the accepted norm of 2:1. Hence, it is not satisfactory. Quick ratio (1.19:1) of the company is more than the standard of 1:1. Therefore, it can be said that the liquid assets are sufficiently available to pay its current liabilities instantly. The cash ratio (0.33:1) is slightly low from the accepted norm of 0.5. Overall, it may be said that the short-term financial position is not sound. The company needs to improve its short-term financial position by paying attention on recovery from debtors and conversion of stock.

2.4.4 Interval Measure

The objective of working capital is to know whether the company is able to meet its daily operating expenses smoothly or not. This objective may be measure by calculating another ratio known as interval measure in addition to current ratio, quick ratio and cash ratio. The interval measure establishes the relationship between liquid assets and average daily operating cash outflow. This ratio examines whether the liquid assets are sufficient to meet daily operating expenses. This can be expressed as:

$$\text{Interval Measure} = \frac{\text{Liquid Assets}}{\text{Average Daily Cash Operating Expenses}}$$

Average Daily Cash Operating Expenses = (Cost of Goods Sold + Administrative Expenses + Selling and Distribution Expenses – (Depreciation + Other Non-cash Expenses) a year

Example 2.2:

The Steel Manufacturing Company is a leading manufacturer of various steel products. The following information has been obtained from the records of the company:

	₹
Cost of Goods Sold	3,00,000
Administrative Expenses (including depreciation)	40,000
Selling and Distribution Expenses	30,000
Depreciation	10,000
Current Assets	1,00,000
Stock	20,000

No. of days in a year 360

You are required to compute Interval measure ratio and comment.

Solution:

$$\text{Interval Measure} = \frac{\text{Liquid Assets}}{\text{Average Daily Cash Operating Expenses}}$$

Liquid Assets = 1,00,000 – 20,000 = ₹ 80,000

$$\text{Average Daily Operating Expenses} = \frac{3{,}00{,}000 + 40{,}000 + 30{,}000 - 10{,}000}{360}$$

$$= ₹\ 1{,}000$$

$$\text{Interval Measure} = \frac{80{,}000}{1{,}000}$$

$$= 80 \text{ days}$$

Comment

It may be said that the company is having sufficient liquid assets to finance its day-to-day operations for 80 days without receiving any cash.

2.4.5 Working Capital Turnover

Assets are used by the company for generating the sales resulting into earning profits which is the ultimate output of a company. Therefore, assets whether fixed and current both should be managed efficiently. The working capital turnover ratio may be calculated for gross and net working capital concepts separately.

(i) Gross Working Capital Turnover Ratio: It may be the objective of the company to know the efficiency of current assets in sales generation. The ratio is also called current assets turnover ratio because the gross working capital is the aggregate of current assets. It is expressed as follows:

$$\text{Gross Working Capital Turnover Ratio} = \frac{\text{Cost of Sales/Sales}}{\text{Current Assets}}$$

The ratio indicates that for generating a sale of one rupee how much investment in current assets is needed.

(ii) Working Capital Turnover Ratio: This ratio indicates how working capital is utilized efficiently in generating revenue. It is also called net current assets turnover ratio and net working capital turnover ratio. High ratio indicates efficient management of working capital and quick turnover of current assets resulting in higher profitability. In other words, the ratio indicates that how much net current assets are needed for sales. The ratio can be calculated as:

$$\text{Working Capital Turnover Ratio} = \frac{\text{Cost of Sales/Sales}}{\text{Average Working Capital}}$$

If cost of sales is not given then the sales figure can be used for the calculation of ratio. Similarly, if opening working capital is not given the net working capital at the end of the year shall be used for the calculation of ratio.

Example 2.3:

The following information are available from the records of Cross Roads Ltd:

	₹
Stock	1,00,000
Bills Receivables	50,000
Debtors	1,50,000
Cash and Bank	20,000
Creditors	1,10,000
Outstanding Expenses	10,000
Cost of Sales	6,40,000

You are required to calculate:

(a) Gross Working Capital Turnover Ratio
(b) Net Working Capital Turnover Ratio

Solution:

(a) Gross Working Capital Turnover Ratio $= \dfrac{\text{Cost of Sales}}{\text{Current Assets}}$

$$= \frac{6,40,000}{3,20,000} = 2 \text{ times}$$

(b) Net Working Capital Turnover Ratio $= \dfrac{\text{Cost of Sales}}{\text{Net Current Assets}}$

$$= \frac{6,40,000}{3,20,000 - 1,20,000}$$

$= 3.2$ times

ILLUSTRATION 2.2: The Balance Sheets of Premier Electronics Ltd. for the years 2020 and 2021 are given below:

Liabilities	*2020 Amount* (₹)	*2021 Amount* (₹)	*Assets*	*2020 Amount* (₹)	*2021 Amount* (₹)
Share Capital	2,50,000	2,00,000	Land and Building	1,00,000	1,20,000
Debentures	1,20,000	1,50,000	Plant and Machinery	1,30,000	1,10,000
Long-term Loans	1,40,000	1,50,000	Furniture	30,000	40,000
Creditors	35,000	30,000	Trade Investments	40,000	30,000
Salaries Payable	20,000	15,000	Stock	1,50,000	1,40,000
Provision for Tax	40,000	50,000	Debtors	1,30,000	1,20,000
Bank Overdraft	25,000	30,000	Marketable Securities	20,000	25,000
			Bank	30,000	40,000
	6,30,000	6,25,000		6,30,000	6,25,000

The cost of sales for the year 2020 and 2021 are ₹ 6,10,000 and ₹ 8,00,000. You are required to calculate:

(i) Current Ratio for 2020 and 2021.
(ii) Quick Ratio for 2020 and 2021.
(iii) Absolute Liquid Ratio 2020 and 2021.
(iv) Gross Working Capital Turnover Ratio for 2020 and 2021.
(v) Net Working Capital Turnover Ratio for 2020 and 2021.
(vi) Working Capital Turnover Ratio for 2021.

Solution:

(i) Current Ratio (2020) $= \dfrac{\text{Current Assets}}{\text{Current Liabilities}}$

$$= \frac{1,50,000 + 1,30,000 + 20,000 + 30,000}{35,000 + 20,000 + 40,000 + 25,000}$$

$$= \frac{3,30,000}{1,20,000} = 2.75:1$$

Current Ratio (2021) $= \dfrac{1,40,000 + 1,20,000 + 25,000 + 40,000}{30,000 + 15,000 + 50,000 + 30,000}$

$$= \frac{3,25,000}{1,25,000} = 2.65:1$$

(ii) Quick Ratio $= \dfrac{\text{Liquid Assets}}{\text{Current Liabilities}}$

Liquid Assets (2020) = Current Assets – Stock
= 3,30,000 – 1,50,000 = ₹ 1,80,000

Quick Ratio (2020) $= \dfrac{1,80,000}{1,20,000} = 1.5:1$

Liquid Assets (2021) = 3,25,000 – 1,40,000 = ₹ 1,85,000

Quick Ratio (2021) $= \dfrac{1,85,000}{1,25,000} = 1.48:1$

(iii) Absolute Liquid Assets = Bank + Marketable Securities
(2020) = 30,000 + 20,000 = ₹ 50,000
(2021) = 40,000 + 25,000 = ₹ 65,000

Absolute Liquid Ratio $= \dfrac{\text{Absolute Liquid Assets}}{\text{Current Liabilities}}$

2020 $= \dfrac{50,000}{1,20,000} = 0.41:1$

2021 $= \dfrac{65,000}{1,25,000} = 0.52:1$

(iv) Gross Working Capital Turnover Ratio $= \dfrac{\text{Cost of Sales}}{\text{Current Assets}}$

2020 $= \dfrac{6,10,000}{3,30,000} = 1.84$ times

2021 $= \dfrac{8,00,000}{3,25,000} = 2.46$ times

(v) Net Working Capital 2020 = 3,30,000 – 1,20,000 = ₹ 2,10,000

2021 = 3,25,000 – 1,25,000 = ₹ 2,00,000

$$\text{Net Working Capital Turnover Ratio} = \frac{\text{Cost of Sales}}{\text{Net Current Assets}}$$

$$2020 = \frac{6,10,000}{2,10,000} = 2.90 \text{ times}$$

$$2021 = \frac{8,00,000}{2,00,000} = 4 \text{ times}$$

(vi) $$\text{Average Working Capital} = \frac{2,10,000 + 2,00,000}{2} = ₹\ 2,05,000$$

$$\text{Working Capital Turnover Ratio (2021)} = \frac{\text{Cost of Sales}}{\text{Average Working Capital}}$$

$$= \frac{8,00,000}{2,05,000} = 3.90 \text{ times}$$

2.5 ADEQUACY OF WORKING CAPITAL

The working capital plays a significant role in the success of business firms. For this purpose, adequate working capital must be available to the firm for running its day-to-day operations as and when needed in required quantity. It does not mean that funds for working capital should be maintained in the firm in sufficient quantity. Such situation may lead to excess working capital which is not in favour of the firm because idle funds earn no profit. On the contrary, if the working capital is not available in required quantity for its operational requirements that may lead to interruption in production activities, loss of business opportunities consequently lowering down the profitability. Such situation may be called inadequacy of working capital. Thus, the working capital should neither be in excess nor inadequate because both the situations are not in favour of the organisation. Therefore, it is a challenge before the finance manager to maintain optimum quantity of working capital all the time in the firm.

Advantages of Adequate Working Capital

The company enjoys the following advantages by maintaining the adequate working capital:

(i) Adequate working capital helps in running the business smoothly resulting into higher profits and maintaining solvency of the firm.

(ii) Solvency helps in enhancing the reputation of the firm. It ensures making due payments in time.

(iii) The regular and in time payments to the creditors develop good relation which helps in obtaining regular supply of raw materials and other inputs on discounts or favourable terms and conditions.

(iv) The adequate amount of working capital ease in meeting daily operational requirements, i.e., payment of wages and salaries and other day-to-day expenses.

(v) The availability of working capital provides uninterrupted production process thereby enabling in meeting the market demand in time and exploiting favourable market conditions.

(vi) External environmental conditions like, slow-down in market, government policies, etc. can be easily faced by the firm having adequate working capital.

Disadvantages of Inadequate Working Capital

The inefficient management of working capital may result into shortage of working capital. If such situation prevails in the business, the firm may face following consequences of inadequate working capital:

(i) The firm shall not be able to meet its day-to-day commitments in time resulting into slow-down in operational efficiency.

(ii) The firm shall not be able to pay its current liabilities in time. This will reduce the goodwill of the firm thereby the firm shall not be able to avail favourable credit facilities from suppliers.

(iii) The fixed facilities like fixed assets cannot be utilised at optimum level due to inadequate working capital.

(iv) Shortage of working capital may result into stoppage of production process due to non-availability of production inputs.

(v) Inadequate working capital will also affect the firm's growth adversely. This will result into not undertaking new and profitable projects and implementing business plans.

(vi) Insufficient working capital may create inefficiencies resulting into insecurity and confidence among employees of the firm.

2.6 DANGERS OF EXCESS WORKING CAPITAL

Excess working capital will lead to lying funds idle in the business that may perpetrate into financial inefficiency. The excess working capital may result into the following consequences:

(i) It may lead to over purchasing of production inputs to avoid shortage. This will result into unnecessary locking of funds in inventories losing use of funds for other productive activities.

(ii) Excessive working capital may have the chances of slackness in the collection of debtors which may result into higher amounts of bad debts.

(iii) Excess working capital means that funds are lying idle in the business. It may lead to loss of opportunity and overall inefficiency in the organisation.

(iv) Unutilised working capital will result into decrease in earning capacity of the firm. It means low rate of return on investments affecting market value of shares.

(v) Excessive working capital may motivate for making speculative profits which is not in favour of the organisation.

In view of the above, it may be said that the finance manager should behave prudently in managing the working capital. Because both the situations, i.e., excess or inadequate working capital are not representing good health of the organisation.

2.7 SYMPTOMS OF POOR WORKING CAPITAL MANAGEMENT

The following symptoms indicates about the poor management of working capital:

(a) Low inventory turnover.
(b) Poor management of creditors, i.e., not making payment in time.
(c) Inefficient collection efforts from debtors will give rise to working capital problems.
(d) Low turnover of finished goods.
(e) Idle funds in the form of working capital.
(f) Dependence of finance manager on financial institutions for financing of working capital needs.
(g) Inefficiency in cash management.

THEORETICAL QUESTIONS

I. Short Answer Type Questions

1. What do you mean by financing of working capital?
2. Define Bond.
3. Explain public deposits.
4. Define trade credit.
5. What do you mean by accruals?
6. Explain commercial paper.
7. Define factoring.
8. What is cash credit?
9. Distinguish between cash credit and overdraft.
10. Define conservative approach of working capital financing.
11. Explain hedging approach of working capital financing.
12. Give the interpretation of current ratio.
13. Define cash ratio.

14. What is interval measure?
15. Explain working capital turnover ratio.
16. Define adequacy of working capital.
17. What are dangers of excess working capital?
18. Give four symptoms of poor working capital.
19. Explain aggressive approach of working capital financing.
20. Explain trade-off between conservative and hedging approaches.

II. Long Answer Type Questions

1. Define financing of working capital. Explain the long-term sources of financing of working capital.
2. What are short-term sources of working capital financing? Explain.
3. Define trade credit. What are its features? Explain the merits and demerits of trade credit as a source of short-term finance.
4. Write notes on:
   (a) Factoring
   (b) Accruals
   (c) Cash credit
   (d) Overdraft
5. Write a note on commercial paper.
6. What are various sources of working capital finance by commercial banks? Explain.
7. What are various approaches to determine an appropriate financing mix of working capital? Also explain the pro and cons of these approaches.
8. Explain the conservative and hedging approaches of working capital financing. Discuss the trade-off between these approaches.
9. Make a comparative study of conservative and aggressive approaches of working capital financing.
10. Among conservative and aggressive approaches which approach is good for working capital financing. Also state the consequences.
11. Explain current ratio, quick ratio and absolute liquid ratio. Are these good for judging the efficiency of working capital management? Discuss.
12. What is meant by working capital turnover ratio? Explain the gross and net working capital turnover ratios.
13. Define adequate working capital. Explain the advantages of adequate working capital and disadvantages of inadequate working capital.
14. What is meant by excess working capital? What are dangers of excess working capital? Explain.
15. Write notes on:
    (a) Distinguish between adequate and inadequate working capital.
    (b) Symptoms of poor working capital.

III. Numerical Questions

1. The balance sheet of Innovative Goods Ltd. as at 31st March, 2023 is as follows:

Liabilities	*Amount* (₹)	*Assets*	*Amount* (₹)
Share capital	10,00,000	Land and building	2,00,000
Reserve and surplus	2,50,000	Plant and Machinery	1,00,000
Long-term loans	4,00,000	Furniture and fixtures	50,000
Creditors	4,00,000	Long-term investments	1,00,000
Bank overdraft	60,000	Stock	7,00,000
Provision for tax	75,000	Debtors	8,70,000
Outstanding interest	65,000	Bank	1,80,000
		Cash	30,000
		Expenses paid in advance	20,000
	22,50,000		22,50,000

Throw light on the short-term financial position of the company with the help of the following ratios:

(a) Current Ratio
(b) Quick Ratio
(c) Absolute Liquid Ratio

Ans: (a) Current Ratio 3:1, (b) Quick Ratio 1.8:1, (c) Absolute Liquid Ratio 0.35:1

2. The following particulars are available from the books of Adarsh Manufacturing Company Ltd.:

		₹
Investment (temporary)		38,000
Inventory:		
Raw material	1,00,000	
Finished goods	1,40,000	
Loose tools	60,000	3,00,000
Book debts		2,00,000
Cash and bank		40,000
Prepaid expenses		10,000
Bills payable		70,000
Sundry creditors		1,00,000
Outstanding expenses		13,000
Overdraft		40,000
Dividend declared		90,000

Calculate and comment on short-term financial position of the company:

(a) Current Ratio
(b) Quick Ratio
(c) Cash Ratio

Ans: (a) Current Ratio 1.88:1, (b) Quick Ratio 0.89:1, and (c) Cash Ratio 0.25:1

3. The working capital of the company is ₹ 50,000. Its current ratio is 2:1. Stock of the company is ₹ 40,000. You are required to calculate:
   (a) Current Assets
   (b) Current Liabilities
   (c) Acid Test Ratio

   Ans: (a) Current assets ₹ 1,00,000, (b) Current liabilities ₹ 50,000, and (c) Acid Test Ratio 1.2:1
4. The following is the balance sheet of XYZ Company Ltd.:

Liabilities	*Amount* (₹)	*Assets*	*Amount* (₹)
Share capital	7,00,000	Goodwill	70,000
General reserve	1,60,000	Fixed assets (net)	8,10,000
Profit and Loss Account	1,50,000	Stock	4,00,000
Long-term loans	4,90,000	Book debts	1,00,000
Bills Payable	40,000	Bills Receivables	50.000
Creditors	1,30,000	Cash at Bank	1,80,000
Interest payable	30,000	Cash in hand	50,000
		Preliminary expenses	40,000
	17,00,000		17,00,000

   The cost of sales of the company is ₹ 58,00,000. You are required to Calculate:
   (a) Gross Working Capital Turnover Ratio
   (b) Net Working Capital Turnover Ratio

   Ans: (a) 7.43 times, (b) 10 times

Part–II

Chapter 3: Inventory

Chapter 4: Inventory Valuation

Chapter 5: Inventory Control

3

Inventory

CHAPTER OVERVIEW AND LEARNING OBJECTIVES

Inventory management is an essential activity especially in case of manufacturing firms. The effective management and control are required due to maintenance of stock levels and involvement of huge investment. A firm has to maintain different types of inventories for smooth running of production process and also fulfilling sales requirements of the market and customers. At the same time, costs are also incurred in ordering and holding of inventories. The holding of inventories also bears the risk of obsolescence, deterioration in quality, etc. For achieving greater efficiency, accuracy and cost effectiveness, the firm has to follow certain inventory management principles. The efficient and effective inventory management provides number of benefits to the organisation. Material loss in the form of waste, scrap, spoilage, defective and obsolete items is also incidental during the production and holding inventories in stock. Therefore, material loss control is essential in maintaining the cost of the product and deciding competitive selling price to match with the market.

Learning Objectives: *The students will be able to:*

- Explain the concept of inventory management
- List the types of inventories
- Estimate inventory costs
- Analyse the risk of holding inventory
- Know the objectives of inventory management
- Discuss the principles of inventory management
- Know benefits of inventory management
- Understand material losses

3.1 INTRODUCTION

Inventory management is an essential activity especially in case of manufacturing organisations. Since the inventory involves high investment of funds for maintaining stock levels and also occupy a significant space of the factory for storage of inventory, therefore, effective management and control is required.

Similarly, inventory is a major element of current assets, i.e., mainly raw materials, work-in-progress and finished goods hence, it should be managed efficiently and proper circulation is needed. Inventory management includes planning for materials purchase to ensure the availability of material in required quantity and quality in the store, organisation of inventory in store in such a way to maintain quality of material as it was purchased, proper handling to avoid wastage and co-ordination with other departments like production, marketing, sales, finance, etc. These are needed to assess the requirement of inventory to production, sales and proper accounting of inventory for exercising effective control and accurate decision making. In other words, efficient inventory management needs to strike a balance between operational requirement and financial requirement. Operational objectives relate to the availability of materials and spares in required quantity and quality as and when needed to avoid disruption in production process. At the same time, finished goods inventory is also necessary to meet the demand of the market avoiding loss of opportunity. On the other hand, finance also pays a significant role in the availability of inventory because of high investment in inventory. The finance department has to ensure the availability of funds as and when required for the purchase of raw materials which is not an easy role. The excess investment or locking of funds should be avoided in the inventory. Thus, inventory management is to focus on maximum efficiency, minimum cost, regular flow of materials to production process and availability of finished goods to meet the sales goal and market demand. In view of this, the stock of raw materials, spares and finished goods are essential because production and sales do not go together. Therefore, inventory is a necessary evil and it requires systematic management.

3.2 INVENTORY

In layman's language inventory means a list of physical items kept in a particular place which is called stores. In a narrow sense, the term inventory is used for stock of goods while in a broader sense, it denotes a detailed list of all physical items of stock. These items used in manufacturing process or rendering services and used for sales having economic value in business activities. As per use or application, inventory differs from business to business. In case of trading organisations, inventory means stock of merchandise held for sale. On the other hand, in a manufacturing organisation the inventory is used in broader sense and includes all physical items used for production, i.e., raw materials, work-in-process, finished goods, spares, consumable supplies, etc. Similarly, in service organisations inventory include sundry supplies used for providing services like lubricants, oils, tools, spare parts, consumables, etc.

Definitions

"Inventory means a schedule of items held at a particular time."–**ICMA**

Accounting Standard 2: Issued by Institute of Chartered Accountants of India defines "inventory as tangible asset held (i) for sale in the ordinary course of business, (ii) in the process of production for such sale, or (iii) in the form of materials or supplies to be consumed in the production process or in the rendering of services."

3.3 TYPES OF INVENTORIES

Accounting Standard 2: States that inventories comprise of:

(a) Goods purchased and held for re-sale
(b) Finished goods produced for sale
(c) Work-in-progress
(d) Material, maintenance supplies, consumables and loose tool awaiting for use in the production process.

But inventories do not include machinery spares items termed as fixed assets and use is not regular.

Thus, in broader sense, inventories in manufacturing organisation include the following:

3.3.1 Raw Materials

Raw material is the basic substance which is major form of input supplied to production process for converting them into finished products. For example, wool, copper, cotton, wood, etc.

3.3.2 Work-in-Progress

It is the stage of semi-finished goods in the production process. It requires further processing for converting into finished products. The quantum of work-in-progress depends on the time of production cycle.

3.3.3 Finished Goods

Finished goods are the outcome of the production process. These goods are ready for sale and provides a buffer between production and market demand.

3.3.4 Spares

Spares are used for the maintenance purposes of machines, vehicles, equipment, etc. Spares play a significant role in ensuing smooth running of machines. Non-availability of spares may lead to shutting of machines resulting into stoppage of production process. The examples are nut, bolts, spring, bearing, etc.

3.3.5 Tools

Tools are also important for the maintenance of machines. These are such as hammers, screwdrivers, drillers, cutters, etc.

3.3.6 Sundry Materials or Consumables

Sundry materials or consumables are used for cleaning and lubricating purposes of plant and machinery and other equipment. These consumables do not require significant investment. Examples of consumables are cotton, sand paper, soap, oil, grease, etc.

3.3.7 Packing Materials

Packing materials are used for housing the finished products for easy handling and safety purposes. Examples are bottles, tins, polythene bags, cartoons, etc.

3.4 INVENTORY COST

The following cost are incurred in ordering or purchasing and carrying or storing the inventories:

3.4.1 Capital Cost

The funds invested in inventories have some costs which is known as capital cost or cost of financing. The carrying of inventories in stores results into locking of funds. Financing may be done from internal sources, i.e., retained earnings and external sources, i.e., borrowed funds. In both cases, the firm incurs cost in the form of opportunity cost or in the form of interest to be paid on borrowed funds. Therefore, efforts should be made by the management in reducing the capital cost as for as possible by maintaining the optimum level of inventories.

3.4.2 Ordering Cost

Ordering cost is the cost which is incurred on purchase of raw materials. Ordering cost includes the clerical and administration costs related to purchase of raw materials. In other words, it includes the cost of processing the order, follow up of order, receiving and inspection and transportation to stores, etc. The ordering cost moves in direct proportion of number of orders. This cost is also called non-carrying cost. It is the aggregate of variable and fixed expenses. Fixed expenses are related to the establishment, rent, salary, etc., of the purchase department.

3.4.3 Storage Costs

All materials purchased from time to time are not consumed by the production process at the same time. Therefore, there is a need for storing the material at a particular place in the factory. This particular space is called stores. The expenses which are incurred in storing and handling of materials is known as storage cost. It is also known as carrying or holding cost. Storage costs include godown rent, insurance, salary of personnel employed in stores, housing equipment, heating and lighting, damage, etc. Similarly, handling costs include the movement cost of materials, placing cost, etc.

3.4.4 Stockout Costs

The objective of the firm is to maintain the regular supply of raw material to the production process in required quantity and quality as and when needed. Similarly, finished goods should also be available in sufficient quantity to meet the demand of customers and market. Out of stock will lead to either stoppage of production process or loss of opportunity in the market. In such situation, extra costs will have to be incurred for emergency purchases of raw materials to avoid the danger of stoppage of production. Such costs may be high price, high freight, no discounts, etc.

3.4.5 Overstocking Costs

Overstocking of materials and finished goods is not in favour of the firm. Overstocking costs are the carrying cost of the inventory in the stores and results into increase in this cost. Such costs are capital cost, handling cost, storage cost, equipment cost, warehouse cost, obsolescence cost, clerical cost, etc.

3.5 NEED FOR HOLDING INVENTORY

In order to harmonise production process and sales requirements of the market and customers, the need for holding inventories arises. Raw materials are input for the production and finished goods are the output of the production for ensuring supply of finished goods on a regular basis to the market. In both the situations, the firm has to hold inventories in sufficient quantity. The objectives or need for holding inventories are:

3.5.1 Transaction Motive

Transaction means purchase of raw materials and sale of finished goods. Transaction motive emphasises on the continuous availability of raw materials to the production process and to facilitate sales operations. Therefore, there should not be non-availability of raw materials in required quantity any time to the production process because there is a time lag between demand of materials and supply of materials. Similarly, stock of finished goods has also to be maintained for meeting regular market demand and also sudden demands of customers.

3.5.2 Precautionary Motive

It is not essential that raw materials will be available in the market in required quantity and quality or specification all the time. If the material could not be procured whenever it is needed from the market, it may lead to stoppage of production process. Therefore, for uninterrupted production activity, the firm is required to maintain adequate stock of materials. The motive also necessitates the holding of inventory for meeting unpredictable changes in the price of raw materials and supply of raw materials. On the other hand, stock of finished goods should also be maintained in adequate quantity to meet the market demand and to avoid risk of unpredictable changes in the sudden demand of the product. Stock of finished goods is also necessary because production and sales are not instantaneous.

3.5.3 Speculative Motive

Speculative motive motivates to take the advantage of price fluctuations, saving in ordering cost, quantity discounts, etc. This motive is used specially in case of seasonal availability of materials. The motive shall be exercised depending upon the availability of funds and space for keeping the extra materials along with housing equipment required as per the nature of material.

In addition to the above causes, there are other causes of holding raw material, work-in-progress and finished goods. These causes are elaborated below:

3.5.4 Reasons for Holding Raw Materials

The following are the causes of holding raw materials in stores:

(i) Daily purchase of raw materials is not possible to meet the daily need of production.

(ii) Quantum, quality and frequency of use in production.

(iii) Distantly located source of supply.

(iv) Procurement of material involve lead time.
(v) Disadvantages of price discounts due to small lot purchasing.
(vi) Seasonal advantage cannot be availed.
(vii) Frequent purchase will increase ordering cost.
(viii) Avoiding risk of contingencies like transport strike, delayed supply by supplier, short supply, etc.

3.5.5 Reasons for Holding Work-in-Progress

The work-in-progress is the result of continuous production process and period of production cycle. The following are the reasons for holding work-in-progress:

(i) Even flow of production
(ii) Continuous use of machines
(iii) Even out the imbalance in demand and supply position

3.5.6 Reasons for Holding Finished Goods

Finished goods are end product of production process. The following are the causes of holding finished goods in stock:

(i) To avoid inability to meet delivery orders in time.
(ii) To meet market demand.
(iii) To meet extra orders if any.
(iv) To avoid loss of goodwill.
(v) To avoid the loss of opportunity.
(vi) To meet unpredictable market/customer demand.

3.6 RISK OF HOLDING INVENTORIES

Risks involved in holding of inventories are as follows:

3.6.1 Risk of Price Decline

There are always chances of fluctuation in the price of materials. Price will not remain the same throughout the period of production. Reduction in prices of materials may be due to increased market supplies, competition in the market, depression in the market, etc.

3.6.2 Risk of Obsolescence

The inventories of raw materials and finished goods may become obsolete due to change in fashion, taste and requirements of the customer and due to improved technology of production. This obsolescence will result into the loss for the organization which is to be avoided.

3.6.3 Risk of Deterioration in Quality

It is the responsibility of the storekeeper to keep the materials in the same state as it was purchased. But after due efforts, the quality of materials may deteriorate by keeping in stores for a long time. Sometimes it happens because of the nature of materials, e.g., wet due to absorption of moisture, spoilage, etc.

3.6.4 Risk of Loss of Material

Loss of material is the incidental to the storage and manufacturing process. Waste, scrap, spoilage, defective will arise in one form or other. The loss may be visible and invisible. Visible loss can be identified like smoke, dust, gas, etc. Invisible loss cannot be seen and the presence of which cannot be identified like shrinkage, evaporation, pilferage, etc. Therefore, proper efforts should be made to reduce the loss of material as far as possible.

3.7 OBJECTIVES OF INVENTORY MANAGEMENT

The main objective of inventory management is to ensure uninterrupted production process and availability of finished goods for meeting market demand and customers demand in time. Inventory is a major element of current assets and involves large investment. Therefore, inventories should be managed efficiently to avoid locking of funds. What is desired is the maintenance of optimum quantity of stock of materials and finished goods and optimum investment in inventories. In other words, carrying cost, ordering cost and risk of obsolescence should be minimised as far as possible. Thus, the objective of inventory management is to achieve maximum efficiency in production and sales with least investment in inventory. Objectives of inventory management are:

3.7.1 Availability of Raw Materials

It is the responsibility of the storekeeper to ensure the supply of raw materials and other materials to the production process as and when required in the required quantity and quality. It does not mean that stock of materials should be maintained in more than the requirement in the store.

3.7.2 Availability of Stock of Finished Goods

In order to match with the reasonable expectations of the customers and unpredictable situation of the market, the stock of finished goods must be maintained in sufficient quantity in the store. This is also essential for regular execution of orders in time.

3.7.3 Economic Purchasing

A proper system has to be developed by the purchase department for the purchase of materials so that the cost of purchase of the material could be maintained at desired level. Thus, the size of the order should be decided in such a way that could ensure the purchase of raw materials at lower cost by availing quantity discounts, reduction in transportation cost, etc.

3.7.4 No Understocking

It is the objective of the inventory control that the stock of raw materials and stock of finished goods both must be available in sufficient quantity. Shortage of raw materials will lead to stoppage of production process and shortage of finished goods stock will lead to loss of opportunity in the market. Both the situations are not in favour of the organization. Therefore, efforts should be made to ensure the availability of both stocks, i.e., raw materials and finished goods.

3.7.5 No Overstocking

The overstocking will lead to the excessive investment in materials and chances of obsolescence of the stock due to change in fashion, taste of customers, etc. Therefore, efforts should be made for optimum investment in inventory and in identifying the slow-moving stock.

3.7.6 Effective Use of Funds

The funds must circulate in the business. This requires the effective management of operating cycle concept of working capital. Therefore, financing of purchases, manufacturing cycle, sale of goods and collection from debtors must be managed effectively. This will ensure proper circulation of funds and generation of surplus for the business. For this purpose, investment in inventory should be at optimum level.

3.7.7 Minimisation of Material Loss Risk

This is another important objective of inventory control. So far as possible risk of loss of material should be minimised so that material cost could be managed effectively. Possibility of material loss may be in the form of obsolescence, shrinkage, evaporation, theft, pilferage, wastage, etc. These losses should be minimized as far as possible.

3.7.8 Furnishing of Data

The cost accounting department has to provide update reports to the management about purchases and consumption stock of materials on regular basis. This will facilitate the short-term and long-term planning and evaluation of inventory control methods and remedies for future.

3.8 PRINCIPLES OF INVENTORY MANAGEMENT

Inventory management is an important aspect of all types of business organisations. It ensures the availability of materials and other inputs in right quantity and quality to production process and also sufficient quantity of finished goods to fulfil customers and market demand in time. Effective and efficient inventory management may assist in optimising costs and improving customers satisfaction. This will ultimately enhance overall business efficiency and reputation resulting into more profits. Thus, for achieving greater efficiency, accuracy and cost effectiveness following principles have to be taken into consideration in their inventory management operations:

3.8.1 Co-ordination among Departments

Inventory management is an important and crucial aspect of manufacturing business operations and its efficiency is largely depended on the co-operation and co-ordination among different departments like purchase, production, sales, marketing, finance, accounts, etc. For example, continuous availability of materials to production department is the responsibility of purchase department which requires co-ordination and co-operation among purchase and production departments. Similarly, co-ordination and co-operation among production and sales department will help in timely execution of sales order.

3.8.2 Raw Material Demand Estimation

Raw material demand estimation is an essential part of a manufacturing organisation. Accurate demand can be assessed with the co-operation of production department. Demand variability should also be addressed to avoid stockout or overstocking taking into account seasonal variations and market trend.

3.8.3 Determination of Stock Levels

In order to avoid excess or shortage of inventory in stores, it is necessary to set different levels of materials like maximum, minimum, re-order level, danger level, etc., to help the purchase department and stores department in purchasing and storing of materials.

3.8.4 Purchasing and Replenishment of Raw Materials

It is the duty of purchase department for accurate order and timely procurement of materials. Ordering quantity, economic order quantity, re-ordering point, lead time and safety stock should be determined by the purchase department on the basis of past data, experience, and future production output. For timely replenishment, follow up of purchase order is needed from the supplier. It provides safety against the disruption in the production process due to non-availability of materials in time.

3.8.5 Storage Management

After the receipt of materials in stores, the materials are placed in appropriate locations in the stores. The objective is to avoid theft, mishandling, loss in storing, and maintenance of materials in good condition and quality. For optimise picking and strategic placement, each item of material should be assigned a name and code. In order to ensure inventory accuracy in stores, the conduct of regular cyclical counting is needed to verify inventories accuracy.

3.8.6 Issue Management

Issue of materials from stores is a crucial activity of inventory management. An appropriate good system is to be installed in the stores to ensure availability of material to the production department in right quantity, quality and at the right time. All the issues should be properly authorised by the authoritative person of requisition department.

3.8.7 Use of Standard Forms

Use of standard forms is essential to provide real time update into inventory levels, location and movements so that decision could be taken by the management relating to future demand and adjust inventory levels accordingly. These standard forms related to purchase, storing and issuing of materials will also help in proper accounting. These forms may be Purchase Requisition, Purchase Order, Bin Card, Stores Ledger, etc.

3.8.8 Valuation of Inventory

The different methods for inventory valuation like FIFO, LIFO, Weighted Average, Standard Price, etc., are considered by different organisations as per their nature and requirement. Materials are purchased at different intervals and issued to production department at different intervals. The valuation of inventory affects material cost as well as the cost of product. Therefore, proper care has to be taken by the cost accountant in valuing the inventory by using appropriate method of pricing so that price charged should be near to market price.

3.8.9 Finished Goods Demand Forecasting

Accurate production of goods largely depends upon the demand of finished product in the market or sales forecasting. The production schedule is carried as per the demand of the product for sale from time to time. Accurate prediction for future demand of the product may be made on the basis of past data, market trend in future, seasonal factors, market research, etc. Therefore, it is essential that demand of finished product should be assessed before the start of production.

3.8.10 Warehouse Management

A proper space and environment have to be provided in the factory for keeping finished goods in good condition. For optimising efficiency, warehouse operations like receiving, placing, handling, packaging, shipping, etc., should be managed properly. Similarly, warehouse layout, equipment utilisation, labour allocation, etc., should also be managed properly.

3.8.11 Supply Chain Management

Supply chain management for procuring materials and supplying finished goods should be appropriately monitored. It should offer end-to-end visibility which requires proper collaboration with suppliers, distributors, retailers, etc., Similarly, transport management should also provide end-to-end visibility about the movement and a contingency plan should also be developed to mitigate supply chain disruptions due to natural calamities, supplier's failure, transport strike, etc.

3.8.12 Risk Management

The various risks are involved in holding inventories like risk of price decline, risk of obsolescence, risk of deterioration in the quality and risk of loss of material. An appropriate action is needed to minimise these risks by the management so that loss of materials and possibility of becoming obsolete of finished goods due to change in fashion or preferences of customers could be reduced. Therefore, demand signals should be monitored and stock of inventory should be adjusted accordingly.

3.8.13 Accounting of Inventory

An effective accounting control system should be in operation for proper records maintenance and accounting of inventories. It includes proper recording of receipt and issue of inventory, material returned, loss of material, pricing of material, etc. Hence, safeguarding the firm's property by proper accounting. Accounting of inventory will also assist in determining accurate cost of product and selling price. Further, real time data will also be available to the management for the purpose of decision making.

3.8.14 Co-ordination in Departments

The co-operation and co-ordination among various departments is essential for the efficient and effective inventory management. This will facilitate proper adherence to above principles. These departments are materials, production, marketing, sales, finance and accounting departments.

Thus, by adhering to these principles, the firm can effectively manage its inventory management operations like cost effectiveness, improvement in customers' satisfaction, enhancing overall operational efficiency, etc.

3.9 BENEFITS OF INVENTORY MANAGEMENT

In today's scenario, inventory management has now become an essential part in production process management because inventory contributes significantly in the total product cost management. An efficient and effective inventory management provides the following benefits:

(i) The inventory management ensures uninterrupted production process by the availability of raw materials in right quantity and quality and at the right time.

(ii) Material resource planning helps in economy in purchasing, storing and issuing materials to production process.

(iii) Material losses in the form of handling of materials, evaporation, pilferage, theft, etc., are minimised with the effective stores management.

(iv) Effective stores management helps in reducing ordering and carrying costs by optimise use of storage space.

(v) Inventory management ensures economy in use of inventory and contributes significantly in reducing the cost of material in the total cost of the product resulting into increase in the profitability of the firm.

(vi) Inventory management reduces the possibility of overstocking and stockout costs. It also reduces the risk of obsolescence and paying high price for emergency purchases to avoid shortage of material to production process.

(vii) Efficient inventory management ensures optimise resources utilisation and improves cash inflow thereby optimise investment of funds in inventory. Thus, enhance the liquidity and availability of cash which can be used for other productive purposes or business operations.

(viii) Demand forecasting matches production schedule and sale operations. It ensures timely execution of sales orders and meeting demand of the market and improving customers satisfaction and loyalty.

(ix) The preparation of proper accounting records provides real time data to the management as and when needed for decision making. It helps in taking strategic decisions and making Planning for future.

(x) Inventory management ensures inventory accuracy in the stores by applying the different techniques of inventory control like perpetual inventory system, cyclical counting, ABC analysis, economic order quantity, determination of stock levels, etc.

3.10 ROLE OF INVENTORY MANAGEMENT

Inventory management plays a significant role in different types of organisations. These roles are:

(i) Ensures scientific purchase of raw materials.

(ii) Minimises the possibility of stockout and overstocking of raw materials and finished goods.

(iii) Minimises storage loss in handling, evaporation, shrinkage, deterioration in quality of raw materials by using proper housing equipment.

(iv) Ensures timely execution of sales order and improves customers satisfaction and loyalty.

(v) Reduces the risk of obsolescence of raw materials as well as finished goods due to change in fashion, preferences and demand of customers.

(vi) Ensures effective use of funds by keeping investment in inventory at optimum level.

(vii) Effective management and control of material losses.

3.11 MATERIAL LOSS MANAGEMENT

Normal loss of material is incidental to the production process. The loss may arise one form or the other like waste, scrap, spoilage and defectives. There is always a difference between the quantity of material entering a job or process and the quantity that comes out in the form of output or products. This can be presented with the following equation:

$$\text{Input} - \text{Output} = \text{Loss}$$

The loss may be visible or invisible. Visible loss can be seen and can be identified like smoke, dust, gas, etc., while the invisible loss cannot be seen and cannot be identified like evaporation, shrinkage, etc. The invisible loss is a waste but the visible loss can be collected or not collected. Further, the loss which cannot be collected is a waste while the loss which can be collected may be usable and may not be usable. The usable loss which can be rectified is called defective and which cannot be rectified is called spoilage. The unusable loss can be sold as scrap and if cannot be sold, it is a waste.

Forms of material loss

The material loss may be in the following forms:

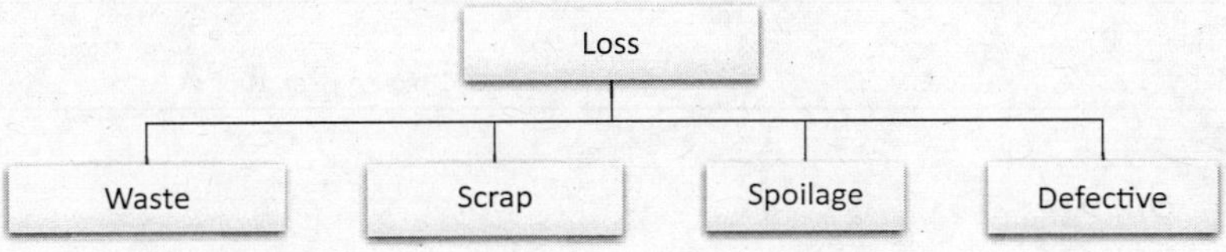

3.11.1 Waste

This is the residue which arises in the course of manufacturing or storage and practically has no recovery value. The waste is invisible and cannot be collected and sold. This arises on account of evaporation, shrinkage, chemical rection, etc. According to the **Cost Accounting Standard-6**, waste means "material lost during production or storage and discarded material which may or may not have any value." The wastages are of two types:

(i) **Normal Wastage:** Normal wastage is natural inevitable and incidental to production process because of nature of material or nature of manufacturing process. Thus, it is unavoidable. Actual waste should be compared with the standards set and if it is near to standard then considered as normal waste. The normal wastage is treated as part of production and therefore, it is added in the cost of the production.

(ii) **Abnormal Wastage:** In simple language, the waste which is in excess of normal waste is called abnormal waste. It occurs due to abnormal reasons, i.e., theft, fire, careless handling, etc. It can be avoided and therefore, it is not treated as a part of production cost. The abnormal wastage is transferred to Costing Profit and Loss Account.

Control of Waste

In order to control the waste of material whether normal or abnormal, a waste report is to be prepared periodically. Then the comparison is to be made between the standard set and the actual waste and the reasons for variance has to be find out so that corrective measures could be taken to prevent them from recurring. The proforma of Waste Report is given below:

PROFORMA

WASTE REPORT

Dept.			No.	
Cost Centre			Date	
Processor Job No.	Actual Waste Qty.	% of the Actual Waste	% of Normal Waste or Standard Set	Remarks
Action taken by				
Entered by			Signature of the Inspector	

3.11.2 Scrap

This is in the form of incidental material residue coming out of certain types of manufacturing process. It is usually in small amount and has low measurable, utility or market value recoverable without further processing. For instance, while manufacturing furniture wooden dust from wood is generated which cannot be reused. According to **CAS-6**, scrap means "discarded material having no or insignificant value and which is usually either disposed of without further treatment (other than reclamation and handling) or re-introduced into the process in place of raw material." It is also unavoidable. It may arise due to normal or abnormal causes.

Types of Scrap

The scrap may be classified into the following types:

(i) **Legitimate Scrap:** This scrap which is incidental to the manufacturing process and is expected or predetermined is known as legitimate scrap, e.g., saw dust, foundry waste. It cannot be avoided but can be minimised with extra efforts. Therefore, it is called normal scrap.

(ii) **Administrative Scrap:** The scrap arising out of the administrative decisions is known as administrative scrap such as change in design, change in technology, etc. It can be avoided but has nominal value.

(iii) **Defective Scrap:** This type of scrap arises due to inferior quality of material, negligent handling of machines, inefficiency of workers. It is the result of avoidable causes. Therefore, it is called abnormal scrap.

Accounting Treatment of Scrap

(i) **Sale Value Credited to Profit and Loss Account:** In this method, amount realised from sale of scrap is credited to the Profit and Loss Account under miscellaneous receipts. The unit cost of production is inclusive of cost of scrap since it is negligible in value (legitimate and administrative scraps). But this treatment is not considered as practical because any value received from the sale of scraps must be dealt with unit cost, i.e., unit cost may be reduced with the value received.

(ii) **Credited to Overhead or Material Cost:** In this method, the scrap is assigned a cost which is usually the sale value less selling and distribution cost. This may be deducted from the factory overhead or material cost. It is useful when several production orders are commenced at a time and not possible to identify scrap for each production order.

(iii) **Credited to Job or Process Responsible for Scrap:** In this method, the realisable value of scrap is credited to the concerned job or process to which scrap is belonged. This method reduces the cost of production with the realisable value of scrap.

(iv) **Transfer of Scrap to Other Job:** Scrap arising in one job may be used for utilisation in another job. Credit should be given where scrap arises and debit should be given to the job using the scrap.

Control of Scrap

In order to control scrap a norm has to be fixed by the organisation which will serve as a control tool. A scrap report has to be prepared from time to time and compare the actual scrap with standard or norm already fixed. In this way, normal scrap and abnormal scrap have to be segregated and corrective action should be taken to minimise the normal scrap and avoid the abnormal scrap from recurring. The proforma of Scrap Report is given below:

PROFORMA

SCRAP REPORT

Dept. .... No. ....

Cost Centre .... Date ....

Process or Job	Scrap Tag No.	Actual Scrap Qty.	% of Actual Scrap	% of Normal Scrap	Abnormal Scrap		Action Suggested
					Qty.	Value	

Action taken by...........

Entered By......... Signature of Inspector

3.11.3 Spoilage

The material damage in the manufacturing process which cannot be rectified or sold as seconds is called spoilage. Spoilage involves not only loss of material but also of labour and factory overheads incurred up-to the stage when spoilage was occurred. According to the **CAS-6**, spoilage means "production that does not meet the quality requirements or specifications and cannot be rectified economically." Thus, the spoilage arises as a result of some defect in the production.

Accounting Treatment of Spoilage

(i) **Normal Spoilage:** The normal spoilage is inherent to the production process and is uncontrollable in the short run. The cost of normal spoilage is a production cost and so it is added.

(ii) **Abnormal Spoilage:** The spoilage more than the normal spoilage is known as abnormal spoilage. It arises due to inefficient production, abnormal causes and therefore, it is controllable. The cost of abnormal spoilage is not born by the production and it is transferred to Costing Profit and Loss Account.

Control of Spoilage

There is a need to control the abnormal spoilage which arises due to abnormal causes like inefficiency of labour, etc. For this purpose, the causes of abnormal spoilage have to be identified and corrective action is to be taken for preventing them from recurring. Therefore, a spoilage report has to be prepared from time to time to keep check on it. The proforma of Spoilage Report is given below:

PROFORMA

SPOILAGE REPORT

Dept. .... No. ....

Cost Centre .... Date ....

Process or Job	Units Produced	Units Spoiled	Normal Spoilage		Abnormal Spoilage		Remarks
			%	Qty.	%	Qty.	

Action taken by ....

Entered by .... Signature of Inspector

3.11.4 Defectives

This is the production which is not meeting the quality standard, specification and norm. It can be rectified by additional processing and sold as first or second in the market and if it cannot be rectified then it will be rejected. According to **CAS-6**, defective means "materials, products or intermediate products that do not meet quality standard." This may include rework which means "defectives which can be brought up-to the standard by putting in additional resources" and reject which means "defectives which cannot meet the quality standards even after putting in additional resources." The reasons for defectives may be poor quality of raw material used, inefficiency of labour, mishandling of plant and machinery, improper product design, etc.

Accounting Treatment of Defectives

(i) If the defective production is identified with a specific job or department, the cost of rework is charged to that specific job or department.

(ii) If the defective production cannot be located to a particular job or department, the cost of rework/rectification is charged as factory overhead.

(iii) If the defective production is due to the abnormal reasons which can be avoided, the rectification cost is transferred to Costing Profit and Loss Account.

Control of Defectives

In order to control defectives, standards must be established cost centre wise. Then, actual defectives should be classified in normal defectives and abnormal defectives by comparing with the standard fixed. Reasons for abnormal defectives should be located and corrective action is to be taken to avoid in future production cycle. For this purpose, a defective report has to be prepared by the department or cost centre. The proforma of Defective Work Report is given below:

PROFORMA

DEFECTIVE WORK REPORT

Dept. .... No. ....
Cost Center..................... Date ....

Process or Job	Defective Units	Normal Defectives	Abnormal Defectives	Cost of Rework	Disposable Value of Defectives	Reasons for Defectives and Action Suggested

Action taken by.....................
Entered by..................... Signature of Inspector

3.12 OBSOLETE ITEMS

The materials items deteriorate in quality, become out-of-date due to better design and change in technology are known as obsolete items. In other words, stock items which are no longer required for use in the production or in some other places of the organisation are called obsolete stocks. Finished goods which become out of fashion, have no customer demand in future and no regular demand can be created by sales promotion techniques are known as obsolete finished goods.

3.12.1 Causes of Obsolescence

Obsolete items of materials and obsolete finished goods are the loss to the organisation. The causes of obsolescence are:

(i) Purchase of raw materials in large quantity more than the regular need or overbuying.
(ii) Excess forward buying.
(iii) All of a sudden fall in production capacity.
(iv) Wrong quality or measurement materials purchased.
(v) Change in design of the product or superseded by an improved design.
(vi) Optimistic sales forecasting.
(vii) Slow moving items become obsolete when no longer required or deteriorate in quality.

3.12.2 Disposal of Obsolete Items

Disposal of obsolete items is a loss for the organisation. It requires immediate action for the disposal to reduce the quantum of loss. Disposal of obsolete items is the responsibility of purchase department or reclamation department. Purchase department knows the use of such materials in own concern. In case of obsolete finished goods, the sales department or reclamation department is to take charge of it. Sales department knows the alternative uses or market for the disposal of such items with profit. Therefore, utmost efficiency is needed in disposing of obsolete items with profitability. Disposal can be made in the following ways:

(i) The obsolete items of materials may be put in some alternative productive use within the concern. In this way, bargain loss may be minimised and also save administrative cost. Finished goods can also be disposed of by making a deal in profitable manner.
(ii) The obsolete items of materials which are in good condition may be returned to supplier from whom it is purchased as per the purchase policy of the concern. This method may be used mainly in case of high value items of materials.
(iii) The obsolete items may be sold directly to other firms using the same materials, it requires sincere efforts in identifying alternative firms.
(iv) The large quantity items in good quality may be sold to dealers or through a broker instead of returning to supplier.
(v) Obsolete items may also be disposed of by selling to the firms having wide experience in dealing in seconds or surplus.
(vi) Obsolete items may also be disposed by inviting tenders, public auction or by annual contract if large in quantity.

3.12.3 Control of Obsolescence

Obsolescence of any item of material and finished goods is not good for the organisation. Therefore, proper and constant efforts are needed to keep check on obsolescence in time and contribute in reducing the loss of the organisation. The following steps may be taken into consideration in controlling obsolescence:

(i) The purchase policy should be framed by the management taking into different consideration like material levels, ordering quantity, etc., and external environmental factors.

(ii) Proper co-ordination between purchase department and production department is needed to avoid overbuying.

(iii) Change in design of the product and technology should be assessed in advance which requires co-ordination with research and development department on continuous basis.

(iv) Accurate sales forecasting should be done taking into consideration market research.

(v) Periodical review of all items of materials should be done on regular basis by a qualified person to identify non-moving or slow-moving items.

In addition to the above factors, the following ratios may also be used to assess the storage loss due to obsolescence. These ratios are:

(i) $\text{Storage Loss Index} = \dfrac{\text{Value of Inventory Loss due to Obsolescence}}{\text{Average Value of Inventory}}$

(ii) $\text{Obsolescence Index} = \dfrac{\text{Value of Non-moving Items}}{\text{Total Inventory Value}}$

These ratios may help in measuring the loss due to obsolescence and non-moving or slow-moving items. The remedial measures should be taken by the management in time to avoid such losses and becoming an item into obsolete item.

THEORETICAL QUESTIONS

I. Short Answer Type Questions

1. Define inventory management.
2. Define inventory.
3. Explain types of inventories as per AS-2.
4. What is capital cost of inventory?
5. Explain stockout and overstocking costs.
6. Explain transaction motive of holding inventory.
7. What are reasons for holding finished goods?

8. Is there any risk in holding inventories?
9. Explain any two principles of inventory management.
10. Define waste.
11. Define scrap.
12. What is spoilage?
13. Explain defectives.
14. Define obsolete items.
15. What are causes of obsolescence?

II. Long Answer Type Questions

1. Define inventory management. What are its types? Explain various inventory costs incurred in purchasing, carrying and storing.
2. Is there any need of holding inventories? Explain the motives of holding inventory.
3. Define inventory. What are causes of holding raw material, work-in-progress and finished goods? Explain.
4. What are risks involved in holding inventories? Explain.
5. Describe the objectives of inventory management.
6. What are principles of inventory management? Explain.
7. Define inventory. What are the benefits of inventory management? Explain.
8. Define scrap. What are its types? Explain accounting treatment of scrap in cost accounts.
9. Distinguish between:
   (i) Waste and scrap
   (ii) Spoilage and defectives
10. Define obsolete items. What are causes of obsolescence? How will you dispose obsolete items? Explain.
11. Define obsolescence. How will you control obsolescence? Explain.

4

Inventory Valuation

CHAPTER OVERVIEW AND LEARNING OBJECTIVES

Inventory valuation is an important activity. In financial accounting, it is related to valuation of closing stock of finished goods while in cost accounting, the valuation of raw material, work-in-progress and closing stock of finished goods is significant. Inventory valuation means converting physical quantities of raw materials and finished goods into monetary value. Different methods are used for the valuation. Inventory of raw materials and finished goods both should be available in required quantity. Inventory inaccuracy may result in either stoppage of production process or loss of business opportunity. It may also result in either overstocking or understocking having its own pros and cons. In order to make storing function efficient there is also a need of classification and codification of raw materials. There are different methods of classification and codification which are used by the organisations as per their requirement. To optimise the inventory management, replenishment policy should be framed by the management so that proper decisions could be taken for selecting the appropriate method for replenishment.

Learning Objectives: *The students will be able to:*

- Explain the concept of inventory valuation
- Understand the objectives of inventory valuation
- Apply different methods of inventory valuation
- Know the impact of overstocking and understocking
- Implement strategies for avoiding overstocking
- Know the methods to classify raw materials
- Learn the methods of codification of materials
- Understand the replenishment policy

4.1 INTRODUCTION

Inventory valuation is an important activity for both trading and manufacturing organisations. In case of trading organisation, inventory valuation is the process of valuing unsold stock at the end of the accounting period while in case of manufacturing organisation, inventory valuation does not include only the valuation of finished goods but it also includes valuation or costing of raw materials issued to production process and work-in-progress. Inventory valuation directly affects the determination of cost of goods sold which impacts the gross profit and net profit of the organisation. In financial accounting, the purpose of correct inventory valuation is to reveal the true and fair view of financial statements. On the other hand, in cost accounting the purpose of inventory (material) valuation is to determine the correct manufacturing cost and selling price of the product. Thus, it may be said that in financial accounting mainly valuation of closing stock of finished goods is significant while in cost accounting, the valuation or costing of raw materials, work-in-progress and closing stock of finished goods is significant specially for manufacturing firms. In financial accounting, valuation of inventory, i.e., closing of finished goods is done on the basis of cost price or market price whichever is less while in cost accounting, the valuation of inventory is only done on the basis of cost.

Inventory valuation means converting physical quantities of raw materials and finished goods into monetary value. In other words, inventory valuation is the costing of raw materials consumed by the production department to estimate the cost of material used in the manufacturing of the product. This valuation or costing of materials forms the basis for pricing decisions. The valuation of inventory is done on two occasions—while issuing raw material to the production process which is also called pricing of material issue and when periodic statements are prepared in terms of value of inventory on hand. Over or undervaluation of inventory leads to inflation or deflation of current year profit and profit of the succeeding period as the case may be. Accurate inventory valuation provides necessary information to the management for taking various decisions like, determining cost of product, selling price of the product, deciding inventory levels of both raw material and finished goods, exercising control over the cost of material etc.

4.2 OBJECTIVES OF INVENTORY VALUATION

Inventory is a significant asset for all types of business organisations, i.e., trading, manufacturing and service organisations. The accurate inventory valuation on hand serves the following purposes:

(i) To allocate accurate cost of material, i.e., pricing of material used in the manufacturing of the product.

(ii) To provide realistic basis for the valuation of closing stock of raw material, work-in-progress and finished goods for determining the cost of product and for the preparation of accounting statements.

(iii) To review the stock levels of raw materials and finished goods.

(iv) To determine accurate cost of goods sold and gross profit and net income.

(v) To reveal true and fair view of accounting statements.
(vi) To provide essential information to management for the purpose of decision making.

4.3 METHODS OF INVENTORY VALUATION

There are a number of methods used for the valuation of inventory in financial account as well as in cost accounts. Accounting Standard-2 (AS-2) recommends four methods for the measurement of cost of inventory in financial accounting. These methods are First-in-First Out, Weightage average, Standard cost and Retail method besides Specific Identification method. In cost accounting, inventory valuation includes the pricing or costing of raw material issued to production department. Apart from the inventory valuation methods recommended by AS-2, some more methods are used for pricing of materials in cost accounting. The purpose of selecting a particular method is that the pricing of material should give a realistic value of stock because it has direct bearing on the cost of product and periodic performance statements in terms of value of inventory on hand. The choice of the method should be based on the nature of material and the nature of business. Some of the important methods of pricing (or valuation) of materials issued to production department are discussed below:

4.3.1 Specific Identification Method

This method is used where materials are purchased specifically for utilisation against a particular job, order, service order etc. In other words, this method can be applied where issues can be identified with specific work order. The Accounting Standard-2 states that "the cost of inventories of items that are not ordinarily interchangeable and goods or services produced and segregated for specific projects should be assigned by specific identification of their individual costs." Specific identification cost means that specific cost which are assigned to identified inventory items. The method is also called specific price method, identification cost method and actual cost method.

Merits

(i) The actual cost is charged to the job and not notional.
(ii) Inventory is valued at actual cost at the end.
(iii) The valuation of inventory does not reflect any unrealised profit or loss.

Demerits

(i) The method is not practicable where inventory items are numerous and interchangeable.
(ii) The method is cumbersome because maintenance of separate stores records needs huge clerical work.

(iii) Since the purchases and issues are on continuous basis, identification of purchases and issues with a specific job or work order becomes difficult.
(iv) The method has only a limited application.

Suitable

This method is suitable in cases,

(i) Where job costing is applied.
(ii) Where costly items of low in volume are used.
(iii) Where non-standard items are purchased to meet specific customer order.

4.3.2 First-in-First Out (FIFO) Method

As the name indicates, this method is based on the assumption that materials received first are issued first to the production process. It means the issue of materials are priced in order of their purchases or chronological order. The philosophy of this method is that the oldest stocks are issued first and the inventory is valued at the price of latest purchases. Generally, it is in the practice of the business firms to issue oldest first and similarly, sell the oldest finished stock first. The **ICMA** defines FIFO method as "the principle that the oldest items or costs are first to be used. Most commonly applied to the pricing of issues of materials based on using first the costs of the oldest materials in stock, irrespective of the sequence in which actual material usage takes place. Closing stock is, therefore, generally valued at relatively current costs."

Merits

(i) The method is simple and easy to understand and operate.
(ii) Actual cost of material is charged to the product.
(iii) Oldest materials are issued first which avoids deterioration in the quality of materials and reduces the possibility of obsolescence.
(iv) The closing stock is valued at the price of latest purchases, i.e., nearer to market price.
(v) No unrealised profit or loss will arise using this method because it is based on actual cost.

Demerits

(i) Often more than one price charged for the requisition of material on same date.
(ii) If the prices are not stable, price fluctuations are reflected in the cost of materials sent to production department.
(iii) The using of this method becomes cumbersome when too many changes in price levels occurs.

(iv) The cost comparison of two similar jobs is not possible due to application of different rates of materials.
(v) It requires a lot of clerical work in case of high fluctuation in material prices.
(vi) In period of rising prices, product costs are understated and higher income is reported.

Suitable

(i) The method is suitable where prices are falling.
(ii) The method is suitable for slow moving stock as well as subject to deterioration in quality and obsolescence.
(iii) The method is good in the situation when prices of material do not fluctuate very often or remain stable.

ILLUSTRATION 4.1: From the following information prepare Stores Ledger Account showing the issue of material on FIFO method.

Purchases of materials are made as under:

Jan. 1, 2022	Invoice No. 200	250 kg	@ ₹ 2.00
Jan. 15, 2022	Invoice No. 215	175 kg	@ ₹ 2.20
Jan. 22, 2022	Invoice No. 300	300 kg	@ ₹ 2.20
Jan. 29, 2022	Invoice No. 400	250 kg	@ ₹ 2.30

Issues were made as follows:

Jan. 17, 2022	Req. No. 10	300 kg
Jan. 27, 2022	Req. No. 80	225 kg
Jan. 28, 2022	Req. No. 100	155 kg
Jan. 31, 2022	Req. No. 120	75 kg

Solution:

Stores Ledger Account

Date	*Receipts*				*Issues*				*Balance*		
Jan. 2022	*Inv. No.*	*Qty. kg*	*Rate (₹)*	*Amount (₹)*	*Req. No.*	*Qty. kg*	*Rate (₹)*	*Amount (₹)*	*Qty. kg*	*Rate (₹)*	*Amount (₹)*
1	200	250	2.00	500					250	2.00	500
15	215	175	2.20	385					175	2.20	385
									425		885
17					10	300		610	300		610
						250	2.00		125		275
						50	2.20				
22	300	300	2.20	660					300	2.20	660

(Contd.)

Date	*Receipts*				*Issues*				*Balance*		
Jan. 2022	*Inv. No.*	*Qty. kg*	*Rate (₹)*	*Amount (₹)*	*Req. No.*	*Qty. kg*	*Rate (₹)*	*Amount (₹)*	*Qty. kg*	*Rate (₹)*	*Amount (₹)*
									425		935
27					80	225		495	225		495
						125	2.20		200		440
						100	2.20				
28					100	155	2.20	341	155		341
									45		99
29	400	250	2.30	575					250		575
									295		674
31					120	75		168	75		168
						45	2.20				
						30	2.30				
		975		2,120		755		1,614	220		506

4.3.3 Last-in-First Out (LIFO) Method

This method is opposite of FIFO method. Under this method, the pricing of issues is done in reverse order. The latest receipt of raw materials from the supplier in the stores is issued first for the pricing of materials. It means if the latest lot of material exhausts, then price of earlier lot is issued for pricing of material. The closing inventory consists of the old lots and is valued at price of such lots. Thus, closing inventory value is understated in the statements. The implication of using this method is that in case of rising prices lower income is reported.

Merits

(i) This method is simple and easy to operate.

(ii) Issue prices are near to market price due to issue of latest purchase of materials.

(iii) Product cost will be more realistic because issues are charged at current market price.

(iv) Fixation of selling price will be easy

(v) If a firm wants to show the lower profits and save tax, LIFO method is used.

Demerits

(i) Some times more than one price is charged for pricing a single requisition.

(ii) The method becomes cumbersome if materials are purchased frequently leading to more clerical work and calculations.
(iii) The value of closing stock is not near to market price because it consists of old lots.
(iv) The cost comparison of two similar jobs is very difficult due to different prices are used for different lots of materials.
(v) In case of falling prices, higher profits are reported if current price is lower than the old prices.

Suitable

(i) This method is suitable in case of rising prices.
(ii) It can also be suitable for bulky materials having high unit cost.
(iii) This method is also suitable in the situation of fluctuating pricing because it tends to minimise unrealised gains or losses in inventory.

ILLUSTRATION 4.2: Prepare Stores Ledger Account by LIFO method from the following information:

Receipts				*Issues*		
Date 2022	*Invoice No.*	*Units (kg)*	*Rate (₹)*	*Date 2022*	*Req. No.*	*Units (kg)*
March 1	10	250	2.00	March 19	10	300
March 18	21	180	2.10	March 27	80	225
March 25	34	300	2.20	March 29	260	260
March 28	40	250	2.30	March 31	300	75

10 kg material purchased on March 25, 2022 were found to be defective and returned to the vendor on March 27, 2022.

Solution:

Stores Ledger Account

Date	*Receipts*				*Issues*				*Balance*		
2022	*Inv. No.*	*Qty. kg*	*Rate (₹)*	*Amount (₹)*	*Req. No.*	*Qty. kg*	*Rate (₹)*	*Amount (₹)*	*Qty. kg*	*Rate (₹)*	*Amount (₹)*
Mar.1	10	250	2.00	500					250	2.00	500
18	21	180	2.10	378					180	2.10	378
									430		878
19					10	300		618	300		618
						180 }	2.10		130	2.00	260
						120 }	2.00				
25	34	300	2.20	660					300	2.20	660
									430		920
27					80	225	2.20	495	225	2.20	495

(Contd.)

Date	*Receipts*				*Issues*				*Balance*		
2022	*Inv. No.*	*Qty. kg*	*Rate (₹)*	*Amount (₹)*	*Req. No.*	*Qty. kg*	*Rate (₹)*	*Amount (₹)*	*Qty. kg*	*Rate (₹)*	*Amount (₹)*
									205		425
27						10	2.20	22	10	2.20	22
									195		403
28	40	250	2.30	575					250	2.30	575
									445		978
29					260	260		597	260		597
						250 }	2.30		185		381
						10 }	2.20				
31					300	75		161	75		161
						55 }	2.20				
						20 }	2.00				
		980		2,113		870		1,893	110		220

Distinction between FIFO and LIFO Method

S.No.	*Basis*	*FIFO*	*LIFO*
1.	Basic assumption	Material received first are issued first to production department.	Latest receipt of material is issued first to production department.
2.	Cost of product	Cost of product represents cost of earlier purchases.	Cost of product shows cost of latest purchases.
3.	Closing inventory	Closing inventory is valued at the price of latest purchases, i.e., near to market price.	Closing inventory is valued at the price of old purchases.
4.	In case of rising prices	Higher income is reported due to old cost of materials.	Lower income is reported due to current cost of material.
5.	In case of falling prices	Lower income is reported due to old prices are more than the current prices.	Higher income is reported due to current prices are lower than the old prices.
6.	Tax implication	In case of rising prices tax liability is increased.	In case of rising prices tax liability is reduced.
7.	Accounting statement	The closing inventory value is shown near the current market price hence, no distortion of accounting statement.	The closing inventory value is shown at the old prices of inventory hence, accounting statements are distorted.

ILLUSTRATION 4.3: BP Service Station and HP Service Station follows FIFO and LIFO method for pricing the petrol sold respectively. On 1st January, 2024 both had same quantity of petrol in stock of 4,000 litres @ of ₹ 80 per

litre. During the month of January each service station purchased 4,000 litres petrol @ ₹85 per litre. Sales during the month were 7,000 litres petrol @ ₹90 per litre. Calculate the profit earned during the month and the value of petrol in stock at the end of the month for each service station.

Solution:

Particulars	*BP Service Station (FIFO) ₹*	*HP Service Station (LIFO) ₹*
Opening Stock 4,000 litres @ ₹80 per litre	3,20,000	3,20,000
Add: Purchases 4,000 litres @ ₹85 per litre	3,40,000	3,40,000
Total stock of petrol	6,60,000	6,60,000
Less: Closing stock	85,000	80,000
Cost of sales	5,75,000	5,80,000
Sales 7,000 litres @ ₹90	6,30,000	6,30,000
Profit	55,000	50,000

Working Notes:

Value of closing stock:

BP Service Station 1,000 litres @ ₹85 = ₹ 85,000

HP Service Station 1,000 litres @ ₹80 = ₹ 80,000

4.3.4 Simple Average Price Method

Under this method, materials are issued to the production department on simple average price instead of cost price of the material. The average price is obtained by adding all the unit prices of material on stock before the issue of material and dividing the total by the number of prices. It may be expressed in the form of the following formula:

$$\text{Simple Average Price} = \frac{\text{Total of prices of all lots of purchases before issue}}{\text{Number of prices}}$$

The simple average price does not take into account the quantity of material. The new simple average price is calculated after every fresh purchase is made of that material. The assumption of the method is that when different purchases are made of the same material on different prices and put in the same bin, the identity of each lot is lost and therefore, there is a need to calculate the average price to keep the issue price near the market price.

Merits

(i) The method is simple and easy to understand.
(ii) The method streamlines the effect of price fluctuation of materials.
(iii) The calculation of simple average price is easy.
(iv) The method is useful when purchases of same material are frequent.

Demerits

(i) The issue price represents average price and not the actual cost price.
(ii) The method ignores the quantity of material in calculating simple average price.
(iii) The value of closing stock does not conform the current market price.
(iv) Issue price may give rise to unrealised profit or loss because issues are not at cost price of materials

Suitable

(i) The method is good when prices do not fluctuate much.
(ii) The method is useful when frequent purchases of same materials are made and mix with the old lot.

ILLUSTRATION 4.4: Prepare the Stores Ledger Account from the following transactions on the basis of Simple Average Method:

Receipts				*Issues*		
Date 2022	*Invoice No.*	*Qty. (kg)*	*Rate (₹)*	*Date 2022*	*Req. No.*	*Qty. (kg)*
May 4	100	100	20.00	May 6	12	50
18	200	150	24.00	20	20	100
21	250	100	22.00	25	25	100

Solution:

Stores Ledger Account

Date	*Receipts*				*Issues*				*Balance*	
May 2022	*Inv. No.*	*Qty kg*	*Rate (₹)*	*Amount (₹)*	*Req. No.*	*Qty kg*	*Rate (₹)*	*Amount (₹)*	*Qty kg*	*Amount (₹)*
4	100	100	20	2,000					100	2,000
6					12	50	20	1,000	50	1,000
									50	1,000
18	200	150	24	3,600					150	3,600
									200	4,600
20					20	100	22[1]	2,200	100	2,200
									100	2,400
21	250	100	22	2,200					100	2,200
									200	4,600
25					25	100	23	2,300	100	2,300
		350				250			100	2,300

Working Notes:

1. Average Price = $\frac{20 + 24}{2}$ = ₹ 22

2. Average Price = $\frac{24 + 22}{2}$ = ₹ 23

4.3.5 Weighted Average Price Method

This method takes into account one of the demerits of the simple average pricing method where the quantities of each lot have not been taken into consideration for calculating the average issue price. In this method, the quantities of each lot and price of each lot both are used for calculating the weighted average price of the issue. The quantities received are considered as weights. The weighted average price is calculated by dividing the total cost of materials in the balance column of stores ledger by the total quantities of material in stock. The rate shall be used for the issue of material until a new lot of material is received in stock when a new weighted average price would be calculated. Thus, calculation of weighted average price becomes perpetual. It may be expressed in the form of the following equation:

$$\text{Weighted Average Price} = \frac{\text{Total Cost of Material}}{\text{Total Quantity of Material}}$$

Merits

(i) The fluctuations in the price of raw materials are streamlined.
(ii) The method ensures appropriate valuation of closing stock and reduced the possibility of unrealised profit or loss.
(iii) Issue prices are more reasonable as compared to simple average issue price.
(iv) The cost comparison of two similar jobs is easy.

Demerits

(i) Clerical work considerably increased.
(ii) Material cost does not represent actual cost.
(iii) Issue rates are to be calculated after every purchase of material.

Suitable

The method is useful where price and quantity of various receipts are liable to fluctuate frequently.

ILLUSTRATION 4.5: From the following information prepare the Stores Ledger Account for the month of March, 2022 relating to the receipts and issues of materials on the basis of Weighted Average Price Method:

Receipts				*Issues*		
Date 2022	*Invoice No.*	*Qty. (kg)*	*Rate (₹)*	*Date 2022*	*Req. No.*	*Qty. (kg)*
March 4	50	200	20	March 7	60	100
18	75	300	24	20	100	200
21	100	100	32	25	300	300

Solution:

Stores Ledger Account

Date	*Receipts*				*Issues*				*Balance*		
March 2022	*Inv. No.*	*Qty. kg*	*Rate (₹)*	*Amount (₹)*	*Req. No.*	*Qty. kg*	*Rate (₹)*	*Amount (₹)*	*Qty. kg*	*Rate (₹)*	*Amount (₹)*
4	50	200	20	4,000					200	20	4,000
7					60	100	20	2,000	100	20	2,000
18	75	300	24	7,200					400	23	9,200
20					100	200	23[1]	4,600	200	23	4,600
21	100	100	32	3,200					300	26	7,800
25					300	300	26[2]	7,800	–	–	–
		600		14,400		600		14,400			

Working Notes:

1. Weighted Average Price $= \dfrac{100 \times 20 + 300 \times 24}{100 + 300} = \dfrac{2000 + 7200}{400} = \dfrac{9200}{400}$

$= ₹\ 23$

2. Weighted Average Price $= \dfrac{200 \times 23 + 100 \times 32}{200 + 100} = \dfrac{4600 + 3200}{300} = \dfrac{7800}{300}$

$= ₹\ 26$

Besides the above inventory valuation method, there are some other pricing methods which do not conform to actual cost and inventory is also valued on selling price. These methods are as follows:

4.3.6 Standard Price Method

Standard price is the predetermined price based on the technical estimates. The price is generally fixed by the management taking into account current prices, anticipated marketing trends, purchase and issue of material, storage quantity, carriage inward, supplies, capacity utilisation, discounts etc. Standard prices are fixed for each material. The issues are made at the standard prices fixed irrespective of the market price of the material. The comparison of the actual price and standard price facilitates the checking of the efficiency in the purchase of materials. The difference between the standard price and actual price of purchase results in material price variance. Thus, standard price is neither cost price nor the market price. Therefore, the standard prices are required to be reviewed regularly in the light of current situation.

Merits

(i) The method is easy to operate and reduces clerical work.
(ii) The method helps in determining the cost of material in advance as per material usage.
(iii) The tender or quotation price can be determined easily.
(iv) Market price variance helps in determining the efficiency of activities related to purchase of materials.
(v) The maintenance of stores ledger becomes easy due to recording of standard price.
(vi) Comparison of two similar jobs is easy due to same issue price, i.e. standard price is recorded.

Demerits

(i) Standard price can only be fixed for short period.
(ii) The standard cost and actual cost will not be same either lower or higher that will result into unrealised profit or loss in the valuation of inventory.
(iii) This method does not conform to accepted accounting principles.
(iv) The determination of standard price may involve some amount of subjectivity.

Suitable

The method is not suitable in case of frequent fluctuation in prices of material.

ILLUSTRATION 4.6: Prepare the Stores Ledger Account from the following particulars of the receipts and issues of materials on the basis of Standard Price Method. The standard price of the materials is fixed ₹ 18 per unit. Find out the value of the closing stock and price variance. Explain the treatment of price variance in accounts.

Receipts			*Issues*	
Date	*Qty. (kg)*	*Rate (₹)*	*Date*	*Qty. (kg)*
Jan. 1, 2022	500	20	Jan. 20, 2022	400
Jan. 10, 2022	200	15	Jan. 23, 2022	100

(Contd.)

Receipts			Issues	
Date	*Qty. (kg)*	*Rate (₹)*	*Date*	*Qty. (kg)*
Jan. 22, 2022	400	18	Jan. 24, 2022	200
Jan. 30, 2022	300	22	Jan. 31, 2022	300

Solution:

Stores Ledger Account

Date	*Receipts*			*Issues*			*Balance*	
Jan. 2022	*Qty. kg*	*Rate (₹)*	*Amount (₹)*	*Qty. kg*	*Rate (₹)*	*Amount (₹)*	*Qty. kg*	*Amount (₹)*
1	500	20	10,000				500	10,000
10	200	15	3,000				700	13,000
20				400	18	7,200	300	5,800
22	400	18	7,200				700	13,000
23				100	18	1,800	600	11,200
24				200	18	3,600	400	7,600
30	300	22	6,600				700	14,200
31				300	18	5,400	400	8,800
	1400		26,800	1000		18,000		

Valuation of closing stock at Standard Price = 400 × 18 = ₹ 7,200

Price Variance = Standard Price – Actual Price

= 7,200 – 8,800 = ₹ 1,600 (A)

The variance of ₹ 1,600 be transferred to Costing Profit and Loss Account.

4.3.7 Inflated Price Method

Normal loss of material is incidental to storing the material because of the nature of materials stored. Therefore, this is useful where material suffers loss in weight due to normal or climatic factors, e.g., evaporation, pilferage etc. In such situations the issue price computed is inflated to cover the normal loss of material.

Example 4.1:

Cost of Petrol purchased	10 litre @ ₹ 90	₹ 900
Less: Normal loss due to evaporation@10%	$\frac{1}{9}$	

Inflated Price = 900/9

= ₹ 100

4.3.8 Replacement Price Method

The cost on the date of acquisition refers to historical cost while replacement cost refers to the cost of material on the date of its issue to the production department. This method is also known as replacement cost method. The difference between purchase price of raw material and the replacement price on the date of use is treated as unrealised gain or loss as the case may be. The market price may be called as replacement price. This method is good in period of rising prices. The main difficulty of this method is that at the time of each issue of materials the replacement price is to be determined which is not an easy job. This may also involve some amount of subjectivity.

4.3.9 Realisable Price Method

Realisable price may be interpreted as market price. This method is generally used in respect of finished goods for sale and also for the items of materials in stores. Realisable value may be more or less from the cost of the materials or finished goods. This will result into gain or loss. At the same time, issues are also not based on the cost. The difference in issue prices, i.e., cost price and market price needs adjustment. It is not easy to ascertain realisable price or value for every issue.

4.4 IMPACT OF INVENTORY INACCURACY

The impact of inventory inaccuracy means either excess or shortage of inventory in stock. In case of raw material, it will result into either stoppage of production process or loss in carrying of excess inventory. Similarly in case of finished goods, it will also result into loss of business opportunity or loss in the form of obsolete items. The impact of inaccuracy of inventory may also reveal the mismanagement of investment in inventory. The following are the impact of inventory inaccuracy:

4.4.1 Overstocking

The organisation fixes inventory levels for all types of items of inventory kept in stores. For each item of material a maximum level is fixed which means the quantity of an item of inventory should not exceed the maximum level at any time. If an item of material exceeds the maximum level, it will amount to overstocking. In other words, overstocking means holding the inventory in stock more than the demand of the production department or customer demand. Overstocking is also called surplus stock or inventory. The surplus inventory includes raw materials, finished goods and components.

Causes of Overstocking

Monitoring of stock levels is a continuous process. The following factors may be attributed to the cause of overstocking:

(i) Inaccurate forecasting of production demand for different raw materials.
(ii) Inaccurate forecasting of customer or market demand for finished goods.
(iii) The purchase of raw materials in more than the requirement just to avail the quantity discounts.
(iv) Seasonal nature of supply of inventory motivates to hold the stock more than the demand.
(v) Seasonality also encourages for taking the advantage of low price.
(vi) Slow moving or obsolete items of materials also leads to overstocking of these items.
(vii) Fear of out-of-stock of any item of material encourages to hold the stock more than the need.
(viii) Ineffective promotional marketing or optimistic sales projections may lead to overstocking of finished goods.
(ix) Supply chain disruption may also lead to excess stock just to avoid shortage any time.
(x) Poor inventory management may also be one of the factors for excess inventory.

Effects of Overstocking

Overstocking should be avoided as far as possible due to the following side effects:

(i) Additionally purchasing of material that becomes overstocks and blocks the significant amount of working capital which could be used profitably for some other productive purposes.
(ii) The most immediate and visible impact in keeping excess stock of material in stores reflects in the form of increase in storage costs like, rent, lighting, insurance, housing equipment etc., and also create space problem.
(iii) The overstocking may result in obsolescence of material and finished goods in keeping for long period. Product expiration and obsolete material is a loss to the organisation.
(iv) Excess stock of material may lead to deterioration in the quality of material and loss of material on account of pilferage, evaporation etc.
(v) Overstocking may result into operational inefficiencies on account of proper handling of material and also complicates warehouse management.

(vi) Additional staff will be required for storing, handling, security etc. Thus, the personnel cost will also increase.
(vii) Overstocking will increase the cost of goods sold.

4.4.2 Understocking

Understocking means insufficient inventory in stock to meet the demand of the production department or demand of the customers/market. In layman's language understocking means that there is no stock in the store. In other words, if the material level crosses minimum level and reaches to danger level, it is called understocking or stockout. In this situation, material department is unable to meet current and anticipated demand.

Causes of Understocking

The causes of the understocking are:

(i) Estimating inaccurate demand of material for the production.
(ii) Inaccurate sales forecasting of finished goods.
(iii) Inefficiency in deciding re-order point and re-ordering quantity.
(iv) Wrong estimation of time lag between ordering and receiving of the material.
(v) Short supply by the supplier.
(vi) Rapid changes in market demand.
(vii) Supply chain complexity may also increase the replenishment period of material leading to stockout.
(viii) The objective of the lean inventory strategy is to keep minimum stock to reduce cost. But if the strategy is not managed efficiently, it may lead to understocking.

Effects of Understocking

Understocking is also not good for the organisations. It often becomes quite expensive and the firm may face a situation of loss of opportunity. The following are the effects of understocking:

(i) The understocking may cause operational disruption due to non-availability of material to the production.
(ii) The firm may face situation of cancellation of order or missed the sales opportunities.
(iii) The non-availability of finished goods in time may create customer dissatisfaction and retention of customers will become difficult.
(iv) Non-fulfilment of the demand of the market in time, the reputation of business will suffer.
(v) Loss of business opportunity will also affect income earning adversely.

(vi) Due to understocking of material, the firm has to make an emergency purchase on higher price from local market to avoid stoppage of production.

(vii) The low level of inventory will result into idle production capacity which is a loss to the organisation.

(viii) Understocking will lead to idle labour time due to stoppage of production.

4.5 STRATEGIES TO AVOID OVERSTOCKING AND UNDERSTOCKING

The basic tenet of avoiding overstocking and understocking is the effective inventory management which is a continuous process. If a firm wants to avoid overstocking just to cut the cost, the risk of facing understocking increases and vice-versa. Therefore, a proper balance is to be maintained between over- and understocking. The strategies are to be developed taking into account the requirement of the firm, market dynamics and customer behaviour, The following strategies may be suggested in this regard:

(a) Accurate demand estimation of raw material is essential taking into consideration of production planning.

(b) Accurate demand forecasting of finished goods is also essential taking into account market environment and customer preferences.

(c) Monitoring of inventory levels on regular basis and timely adjustment/arrangement is needed for any excess or shortage of material or finished goods.

(d) A proper care has to be taken while deciding the re-order point, re-order quantity and safety stock quantity.

(e) Seasonality factor should be considered in respect of materials as well as finished goods.

(f) The supplier collaboration is to be maintained to ensure timely supply of material in required quantity and quality.

(g) Similarly, market co-ordination is also needed for positioning in competitive market environment.

4.6 CLASSIFICATION OF MATERIALS

A manufacturing concern needs variety of items of material of different grades, specification etc., for smooth running of production process. These all items are stored in the stores. The efficiency of stores function lies in quick location and identification of materials for the issue. When innumerable materials are stocked in store room, it is not an easy job to locate and identify material in no time. In order to make storing function efficient, there is a need of classification of material. It is a standardised arrangement of materials in stores according to the nature, usage, similarities, values etc. This is mostly required in case of centralised storing system. Classification of material facilitates prompt identification of materials in stores. In other words, classification is the process of arranging items of materials into groups according to their nature, attributes, relations, value etc. By classification of material, control can be exercised efficiently. The basis of classification of inventory should be consistent and remain unchanged. The system of classification should also be flexible and allow reasonable scope for extension or adjustment.

4.6.1 Methods of Classification

Stores are generally classified on the following basis:

1. **Nature:** On the basis of nature, the stores are classified into specific groups. It is a common method which is used by the organisations. The classification of materials and supplies may be done in the following groups:
   (i) Raw materials
   (ii) Work-in-progress
   (iii) Component parts
   (iv) Spares
   (v) Tools
   (vi) Consumable stores
   (vii) Packing materials
   (viii) Finished goods
2. **Usage:** On the basis of consumption of different types of materials, it has been observed that all the materials are not consumed in the same manner. Some materials are consumed on regular basis while others on intermittent basis. On the basis of usage, the materials may be classified in the following categories:
   (i) **Fast moving materials:** The materials whose turnover is high, are called fast moving materials. It means these are regular in use and hence, these should be maintained as per the requirement of the production.
   (ii) **Slow moving materials:** The material having low turnover are called slow moving materials. It means these are not in regular use and hence, there stock should not be maintained in excess. Further, such materials stocks should be reviewed periodically to avoid to become obsolete.
   (iii) **Dormant materials:** The material having no current demand for consumption are called dormant materials. Such materials should be maintained in minimal quantity and should be purchased when the full stock is consumed.

(iv) **Obsolete materials:** The material having no demand for consumption of the production process and there is no demand due to use of substitute material or discontinued in future are called obsolete materials. Such materials after a careful review should be declared as scrap and their value should be realised by selling.

3. **Value:** The different types of materials having different money value are stored in the stores. Stocks are classified on the basis of money value of inventory as follows:

   (i) **High value items:** High value items of materials are those which constitute around 70% of inventory value and around 10% of the total quantity held in stock. Such items need strict control.

   (ii) **Moderate value items:** The moderate value items consist of around 20% of inventory value and around similar percentage of total quantity held in stock. Such items of inventory need moderate control.

   (iii) **Low value items:** Low value items are those which are remaining 70% of the quantity held in stock and 10% of inventory value. Hence, low or no control is required for such items.

4.6.2 Advantages of Classification of Inventory

In order to perform storekeeping function by the storekeeper efficiently, it requires proper classification of various items of inventory stored in stores. The following are the advantages of proper classification of inventory held in stock:

(a) The systematic grouping of materials helps in identifying right material in no time.

(b) The systematic grouping of similar items also helps in reducing the size and varieties.

(c) The classification of materials also facilitates in finding substitutes available in the market.

(d) The systematic classification makes easier in recording of materials in bin cards and arranging them properly.

(e) The classification of inventory also helps in making correspondence accurately.

4.7 CODIFICATION OF MATERIALS

Codification is the next step in stores control after the classification of materials. The innumerable items of inventory are stocked in the stores having different names of each item. The different suppliers may use short name, full name or different name in practice of the same material. In order to facilitates the purchasing of materials, it would be better to assign a code to the items of materials along-with the name of materials to avoid any confusion among different persons dealing with the purchasing, inspecting, storing etc. of a particular classified material. Coding is the procedure for assigning symbols scientifically to all classified materials stocked in the stores. The code may be numeric, alphabetic and a combination of these two for each item of material. The colour scheme may also be used for the quick identification of materials. The code and colour system will also facilitate to less literate persons working in the stores in quick identification of materials.

4.7.1 Requisites of Coding

The requisites of coding are:

(i) Code should be small but does not mean that it should not be comprehensive.
(ii) There should not be repetition of the same code.
(iii) Only one code for each item should be assigned.
(iv) The code should be easy to understand even by less literate persons.
(v) The code should be flexible to accommodate new additions.
(vi) The code should facilitate mechanised accounting.
(vii) The code number should be self-explanatory to a possible extent.

4.7.2 Methods of Codification

Generally, the following methods are in practice for code construction:

1. **Alphabetic Method:** Under this method, each item of material is assigned an alphabet letter or combination of alphabet letters. In this method, 26 alphabets are used as elements. This method is also known as mnemonic method. For example, alphabet letter 'F' may be used for fertilizer and 'UF' may be designated to urea fertilizer and 'NF' may be used for nitrogen fertilizer. This method can be effectively applied only when the stock items are less in number.
2. **Numerical Method**: As the name indicates, each item of material in the stores is identified by a number or combination of numbers. For example, fertilizer may be assigned 10 number and urea fertilizer 1 and nitrogen fertilizer 2 and so on. In such case, urea fertilizer will indicate the code 10.1 and nitrogen fertilizer will indicate the code 10.2.
3. **Alpha-numeric Method:** This method is the combination of alphabet and numerical method where both alphabet letters and numerical numbers are used for codification. Under this method, alphabet letters may be used for the codification of general class of material and sub-class of material by a numerical number and vice-versa depending upon the convenience of the firm. For example, 'S' denote steel and 'S1' and

'S2' are identified as mild steel and cast steel. The basic advantage of this method is that it is flexible and can be used for large number of items stocked in the stores and also in case of additional new items.

4. **Location Coding:** In addition to the above mentioned methods, a location coding may also be used where the size of the stores is large in area. This will help in identifying the location or bin where a particular item is placed in stores. A number may be given to bin or rack. Generally, block system may be used to designate the location. The block may be named as metal items, liquid items, spares items and so on.

4.7.3 Advantages of Coding

Codification of materials may serve the following purposes:

(i) It facilitates the identification of materials and it will become more easier when code is accompanied by a location code.

(ii) It facilitates the right purchase of material.

(iii) It makes the issue of material quick.

(iv) It saves the time in writing and describing about the material to be purchased.

(v) Coding also avoids the confusion about the material under purchase, placed or issue.

(vi) It facilitates co-ordination between purchase department, stores and production department.

(vii) Codification ensures secrecy as codes are not known by all.

(viii) It reduces the handling time of material in stores.

4.8 LEAD TIME

Purchasing, storing and issuing of materials are the common and recurring functions in a manufacturing firm. Purchasing firm and supplier both require time for processing of order and execution of order respectively. The total of these two times is known as lead time. Lead time refers to the total time required for the whole replenishment procedure. Lead time may be expressed with the help of the following equation:

Lead Time = Time taken for placing an order + Time taken by the supplier for delivery of order

Or = Order Processing Time + Delivery Time

Lead time is usually expressed in number of days. Lead time plays an important role in deciding re-order point. Proper care is to be taken while deciding lead time. If the material has not been received within lead time, it may lead to decrease in safety stock and possibility may also arise of stoppage of production process due to non-availability of material in needed quantity. Thus, lead time is an important tool for inventory planning and control.

4.9 REPLENISHMENT POLICY

The purpose of replenishment policy is to optimise the inventory management and meet the production and customer demand effectively. The various/different issues are considered and decisions are taken for every item of inventory. These decisions are:

(a) The quantity of an order which is to be replenished.
(b) Lead time to replenished the order.
(c) Minimising inventory cost or replenishment cost.
(d) Reducing the possibility of stockout and overstock.

4.9.1 Replenishment Methods

The replenishment methods are strategies to ensure the availability of material to the production when needed in required quantity and quality. The following methods are generally in practice:

1. **Re-order Point Method:** Re-order point decides when an order for the purchase of a material should be placed as per economic order quantity to avoid the stockout and also ensure economical purchase. At this point storekeeper should initiate the process of purchasing a material. Sometimes, it may lead to overstock if the demand is lower than expected.
2. **Lead Time Method:** This method considers the gap between the placing of an order and its subsequent receipt. It focusses on the reduction of lead time to avoid the use of safety stock as well as need of having large safety stock. Thus, it reduces carrying cost and requires constant touch with suppliers for executing order in time.
3. **Fixed Period System:** Under this system, inventory levels are reviewed at fixed interval. Generally, inventory levels are reviewed weekly, fortnightly or monthly as per the need. After the review of inventory levels, ordering quantity is determined and order is placed to bring the inventory level up-to the maximum stock level. The order size may vary after every review. The system requires frequent inventory counts or updated accounting records. The system is good for managing multiple items having varying demand pattern.
4. **Other Methods:** In case of slow-moving items, one-to-one order policy may be adopted. If there is a demand for one unit, purchase of one unit is to be ordered. Similarly, static inventory system may be adopted and one purchase decision will be taken for the entire project duration.

4.9.2 Method Selection

The right selection of inventory replenishment method depends on the number of factors. These factors may be:

(i) Lead time
(ii) Demand pattern
(iii) Inventory carrying cost
(iv) Ordering cost
(v) Stockout cost
(vi) Environmental factors
(vii) Nature of business

After considering the above factors, a proper decision may be taken by the management for selecting most appropriate method of replenishment of material. This will facilitate in meeting production demand in time and also optimise inventory investment.

THEORETICAL QUESTIONS

I. Short Answer Type Questions

1. Define inventory valuation.
2. Explain FIFO method of inventory valuation.
3. Explain weighted average pricing method.
4. What is replacement price method?
5. Define overstocking.
6. Explain understocking.
7. What are the effects of understocking?
8. Define classification of material.
9. Explain codification of material.
10. Explain alphabetic method of codification.
11. Define lead time.
12. What are requisites of coding?
13. What is location coding?
14. Explain replenishment policy.
15. Explain re-ordering point method of replenishment.

II. Long Answer Type Questions

1. Define inventory valuation. Explain the objectives of inventory valuation.
2. Explain the FIFO and LIFO methods of inventory valuation. Under what conditions these methods are suitable?
3. What is weighted average pricing method of inventory valuation? Explain its merits and demerits.

4. Explain standard pricing method of inventory valuation along-with the merits and demerits.
5. Write short notes on:
   (i) Distinction between FIFO and LIFO methods.
   (ii) Replacement price method.
   (iii) Realisable price method.
6. Define overstocking. Explain the causes and effects of overstocking.
7. Define understocking. Explain its causes and effects.
8. Explain overstocking and understocking. What strategies will you suggest for avoiding overstocking and understocking.
9. Define classification of materials. Describe the methods of classification of materials.
10. What is meant by classification of materials? What are advantages of classification of inventory in inventory management? Explain.
11. Define codification of materials. Explain the requisites and advantages of coding.
12. Explain codification of materials. What are different methods of codification? Discuss.
13. Define replenishment policy. Explain the different replenishment methods. What factors have to be considered for right selection of inventory replenishment method.
14. Write notes on:
    (i) Lead time.
    (ii) Specific identification method of inventory valuation method.
    (iii) Distinguish between overstocking and understocking.

III. Numerical Questions

1. Sudarshan Textiles Ltd. provides the following information about purchase and issue of a material:
   April 1 Opening stock of material 1,000 units @ ₹ 10 per unit
   April 2 Purchased 4,000 units @₹ 15 per unit
   April 4 Issued 4,500 units
   April 6 Purchased 5,000 units @₹ 16 per unit
   April 7 Issued 3,000 units
   April 8 Purchased 3,000 units @₹ 17 per unit
   April 10 Issued 4,000 units
   April 15 Refund of surplus from a contract 25 units @ ₹ 10 per unit
   April 18 Issued 1,000 units
   April 25 Issued 500 units
   April 27 Purchased 3,000 units @ ₹ 15 per unit
   April 29 Issued 1,025 units
   The store verifier of the factory noted that on April 30, he has found a shortage of 10 units.

Prepare Stores Ledger using FIFO method of valuing the material issues and compute the value of closing inventory.

Ans: Closing stock 1,990 units, Value ₹ 29,850

2. Prepare Stores Ledger Card using the FIFO method of issue pricing on the basis of the following information:

   Sept. 1 Opening stock 20 units @ ₹ 2
   Sept. 10 Issued 10 units
   Sept. 15 Purchased 30 units @ ₹ 4
   Sept. 20 Issued 30 units
   Sept. 25 Purchased 40 units @ ₹ 5
   Sept. 25 Received back in store 10 units which were issued on 10th Sept.
   Sept. 28 Issued 20 units

   (B.Com. Hons. D.U.)

   Ans: Closing stock units 40 and value ₹ 200

3. The following information are available of a manufacturing unit of a company for material No. S20 for the month of January, 2021:

   2021
   Jan. 1 Opening stock 50 units @ ₹ 4
   Jan. 3 Purchases 100 units @ ₹ 3
   Jan. 6 Purchases 100 units @ ₹ 5
   Jan. 15 Issue 100 units
   Jan. 18 Purchases 150 units @ ₹ 6
   Jan. 24 Issue 250 units
   Jan. 27 Purchases 100 units @ ₹ 6
   Jan. 28 Issue 100 units

   Prepare Stores Ledger using LIFO method.

   Ans: Closing stock 50 units and Value ₹ 200

4. The following transactions relate to the purchase and issue of a material:

   Jan. 2 Purchased 4,000 units @ ₹ 4 per unit
   Jan. 20 Purchased 500 units @ ₹ 5 per unit
   Feb. 5 Issued 2,000 units
   Feb. 10 Purchased 6,000 units @ ₹ 6 per unit
   Feb. 12 Issued 4,000 units
   March 2 Shortage 1,000 units
   March 5 Issued 2,000 units
   March 15 Purchased 4,500 units @ ₹ 5.50 per unit
   March 20 Issued 3,000 units

   Prepare Stores Ledger using LIFO method of pricing of material issued.

   (B.Com. Hons. D.U.)

   Ans: Closing stock 8,000 units and Value ₹ 14,250

5. The following transactions relate to purchases and issue of material of Sugandh Ltd.:
   Jan. 1, 2016 Purchased 300 units @ ₹ 6 per unit
   Jan. 4, 2016 Purchased 600 units @ ₹ 8 per unit
   Jan. 6, 2016 Issued 500 units
   Jan.10, 2016 Purchased 700 units @ ₹ 8 per unit
   Jan.16, 2016 Issued 800 units
   Jan.20, 2016 Purchased 300 units @ ₹ 10 per unit
   Jan.24, 2016 Issued 100 units
   Prepare Stores Ledger if issues are made under the following methods:
   (a) First-in-first out
   (b) Last-in-first out

   (B.Com. Hons. B.H.U.)

   Ans: Closing stock-FIFO 500 units, Value ₹ 4,600. LIFO 500 units, Value ₹ 3,800
6. Bharat Petroleum sold Petrol through Aditi service station and Adarsh service station. Aditi service station follows FIFO method while Adarsh service station follows LIFO method. On 1st January, 2022 both stations have opening stock of Petrol 10,000 litres @ ₹80 per litre. Each station purchased additional supplies of 5,000 litres Petrol @ ₹85 per litre. Sales for each of these stations during the month were 14,000 litres @ ₹90 per litre. Calculate for each service station the profit earned during the month and the value of Petrol in stock at the end of the month.
   Ans: FIFO-Profit ₹1,20,000 and value of closing stock 1,000 litres ₹85,000. LIFO-Profit ₹1,15,000 and value of closing stock 1,000 litres ₹80,000
7. From the following information prepare stores ledger adopting simple average price method:
   March 1, 2022 Purchased 250 units @ ₹4 per unit
   March 7, 2022 Purchased 150 units @ ₹5 per unit
   March 10, 2022 Issued 300 units
   March 20, 2022 Purchased 200 units @ ₹6 per unit
   March 25, 2022 Issued 150 units
   March 28, 2022 Purchased 250 units@ ₹7 per unit
   March 31, 2022 Issued 100 units
   Ans: Closing stock 300 units and value ₹1,875
8. Purchases and issues of a certain material for the month of January, 2023 are given below:
   Jan. 1, 2023 Purchased 200 units @ ₹5 per unit
   Jan. 8, 2023 Issued 160 units
   Jan. 14, 2023 Purchased 200 units @ ₹6 per unit
   Jan. 17, 2023 Issued 200 units
   Jan. 20, 2023 Purchased 100 units @ ₹7 per unit

Jan. 25, 2023 Purchased 200 units @ ₹6.50 per unit
Jan. 31, 2023 Issued 180 units
Prepare stores ledger using weighted average basis of issue price.
Ans: Closing stock 160 units, Value ₹1,051

9. Prepare stores ledger using weighted average method of valuing the material issues from the following details of stores receipts and issues of Material 'A':
March 1 Opening stock 2,000units @ ₹5 each
„ 3 Issued 1,500 units
„ 4 Received 4,500 units @ ₹6 each
„ 7 Issued 1,600 units
„ 8 Returned to stores 100 units by production department from the issue of March 3
„ 15 Received 2,400 units @ ₹6.50 each
„ 18 Returned to suppliers 200 units from the material received on March 4
„ 24 Received 1,000 units @ ₹7 each
„ 26 Issued 2,100 units
„ 27 Received 1,200 units @ ₹7.50 each
„ 31 Issued 2,800 units
Use rate up-to two decimal places. What is the quantity and value of the material consumed in the month of March?
(B.Com. Hons. D.U.)
Ans: Material consumed 7,900 units, Value ₹ 47,842

10. The purchases and issues of Shantanu Ltd. for the month of April are as follows:
April 1 Purchases 200 units @ ₹ 10
April 4 Purchases 175 units @ ₹ 9
April 8 Issues 150 units
April 18 Purchases 200 units @ ₹ 10
April 26 Purchases 125 units @ ₹ 12
April 30 Issues 250 units
The standard price of material is fixed at ₹ 15. Prepare stores ledger adopting standard price for the issue of material.
Ans: Closing stock 300 units, Value ₹ 1,075

5

Inventory Control

CHAPTER OVERVIEW AND LEARNING OBJECTIVES

Inventory control includes proper planning and control of purchasing, storing and issuing of material to avoid wastage and losses. Inventory control refers to the physical control and financial control. For effective control on inventory, there should be proper co-ordination among various departments, economic purchasing of material, efficient stock control and review by the management regularly of all activities. A proper inventory control system helps in reducing the cost of inventory resulting into increase in profits. The various inventory control techniques such as determination of stock levels, economic order quantity, ABC analysis, JIT system, Control ratios, VED analysis etc., are used by the management for effective control over inventory costs.

Learning Objectives: *The students will be able to:*

- Understand the meaning and concept of inventory control
- Know the objectives of inventory control
- Explain essential requirement of effective inventory control
- Know the importance of inventory control
- Apply techniques of inventory control based on the need and nature of material

5.1 INTRODUCTION

Inventory is an integral part of a manufacturing and trading organisations as compared to service organisations. In a manufacturing firm raw materials are the main form of inventory while in trading organisations finished goods, i.e., merchandised are main form of inventory. Therefore, inventory management is most crucial in manufacturing firms for their success. Hence, inventory control is a significant activity in such organisations. Inventory is the largest form of current assets (stock of raw materials, work-in-progress and finished goods) in most of the firms thereby locking-up significant amount of working capital. Inventory control includes physical control and financial control. Physical control means the efficient management of different inventory from planning, procurement, storing and issuing to production process as and when needed in required quantity and quality to ensure smooth running of production process and avoid wastage and losses. Thus, inventory should be maintained in an optimum quantity to avoid over-and understocking and minimise the locking of funds. This is only possible by exercising effective control on inventory. The holding of inventories involves capital and other costs. Therefore, financial control is also essential which helps in reducing the investment in inventory and avoiding excess locking of funds. Thus, the system of inventory control should be comprehensive. According to CIMA (UK), "Inventory control is the systematic regulation of inventory levels." Inventory control is the system of maintaining inventory items at desired level to ensure the even flow of production and at the same time avoid excess investment in inventory. Thus, inventory control is related with the following aspects:

(i) Efficient management of all items of inventory mainly, raw materials, work-in-process and finished goods.
(ii) Maintaining of inventory items in desired quantity to ensure smooth production process.
(iii) Regulating investment in inventory to avoid excess investment.
(iv) Minimising material cost and avoiding wastage and losses.

5.2 OBJECTIVES OF INVENTORY CONTROL

The objectives of inventory control may be classified under two headings:

1. Physical Objectives
2. Financial Objectives

5.2.1 Physical Objectives

The physical objective means that the material and spares must be available in required quantity and quality so that production work should not be disrupt for want of inventory. The physical objectives are:

(i) **Economical Purchasing:** The purchasing of material should be at reasonable or lower price. The purchasing department can contribute significantly by efficient management of quality, quantity and timing of purchase. The 5Rs which mean right quantity, right quality, right price, right time, and right supplier should be taken into consideration while purchasing raw material.
(ii) **Availability of Material:** The availability of materials should be continuous in required quantity, quality and time so that uninterrupted flow of material for production could be ensured. At the same time, optimum level of inventory should be maintained in stock.
(iii) **Avoidance of Wastage and Losses:** Materials are subject to deterioration in the quality while keeping in stores for a long time. Such wastages and losses may be in the form of rust, moisture,

breakage, pilferage, evaporation etc. The causes of such losses should be identified and corrective measures should be taken in time to eliminate such wastages and losses.

(iv) **Avoidance of Overstocking:** The overstocking may lead to increase in cost of material like capital cost, storage cost, equipment cost etc. It may also be subject to wastages, losses and obsolescence. Locking of funds in idle inventory will also result in loss of investment opportunity.

(v) **Avoidance of Out of Stock:** It is also the objective of inventory control to ensure the availability of raw material to production process and finished goods for meeting the demand of the market. Out of stock may either adversely affect the production process or demand of the market.

(vi) **Avoidance of Obsolescence:** The inventory either raw material or finished goods may become obsolete due to change in requirement, technology, fashion, customer taste etc. Therefore, market research should be conducted from time to time so that risk of obsolescence should be avoided or minimised.

(vii) **Avoidance of Misappropriation:** Misappropriation or theft of inventory should be prevented specially required in case of high priced and small in size items. It requires proper accounting of inventory, safety of stock and physical verification of stock from time to time so that any discrepancy could be identified and corrective measures could be taken to avoid losses.

(viii) **Availability of Finished Goods Stock:** The finished goods must be available in reasonable quantity in stock to match the expectations of customers, demand of the market and prompt execution of the order. This will help in providing better services to the customers as well as increasing product demand and also meeting the competition in the market.

(ix) **Furnishing of Data to Management:** The cost accounting department has to provide updated reports to the management from time to time about purchases, consumption, stock of raw materials and finished goods. This will facilitate the short-term and long-term planning and evaluation of effectiveness of inventory control methods and taking remedial actions for future.

5.2.2 Financial Objectives

The financial objectives of inventory control mean optimum application of funds in inventory. The financial objectives may be:

(i) **Effective Use of Funds:** The funds must circulate in the business. It requires effective management of operating cycle concept of working capital. Therefore, financing of purchases, manufacturing cycle, conversion of finished goods into sales and collection from debtors must be managed effectively so that minimum working capital should be locked in current assets. This will ensure proper circulation of funds and generation of surplus for the business. Hence, investment in inventory neither should be over or under. A balance approach should be followed to minimise the cost of capital.

(ii) **Minimisation of Inventory Cost:** The inventory cost should be minimised by adopting different techniques of inventory control like fixing materials levels, economic order quantity etc. The optimum investment in inventory will help in increasing the profits of the firm.

5.3 IMPORTANCE OF INVENTORY CONTROL

Inventory control is essentials for all types of business firms because over or understocking of inventory both are not in favour of any business unit. Overstocking leads to locking of funds and cannot be used for other productive purposes while understocking may lead to disruption in production process and loss of business opportunity due to not meeting the market demand in time. The following factors contribute to the importance of inventory control:

(i) **Avoidance of Stockout Cost:** If inventories are out of stock either sales or market demand of the finished goods will be adversely affected or extra cost will have to incur for emergency purchases to meet the requirement of the production process for stockout materials. This is only possible by keeping control over the levels of inventories maintained in the firm.

(ii) **Avoidance of Overstocking Costs:** Overstocking costs are the inventory carrying or storage costs. Storage costs include costs of storing and handling of inventories. These costs can be put under control by proper determination of stock levels of inventories maintained in the store.

(iii) **Increase in Profits:** Inventory control can contribute significantly to the profits of the firm by the efficient management of different costs, i.e., capital cost, stockout costs, storage costs and other costs.

(iv) **Accounting Control:** Accounting control of inventories is concerned with the proper recording of inventory for safeguarding the firm's property in the form of raw materials, semi-finished goods and finished goods. Efficient system of records keeping also increases the effectiveness of the operative and financial control.

(v) **Uncertainty in Replenishment Period:** Replenishment time cannot be said as certain. Supplier may take more time in supplying materials which may sometimes lead to shortage of material. Therefore, it is necessary that adequate inventory has to be maintained to avoid stoppage of production process.

5.4 ESSENTIALS OF INVENTORY CONTROL

In order to keep effective control on inventory, the following essential requirements should be taken into consideration:

(i) There should be proper co-ordination among various departments, i.e., purchase department, production department, stores department, marketing/sales department, costing department etc. of the firm to assess and meet funds requirement, production requirements and market demand.

(ii) Purchasing is a specialised activity which is performed frequently in the manufacturing organisations. Therefore, it should be performed by the purchase department under the control of competent purchase officer.

(iii) For the proper planning of material requirements, a list of all materials used in production should be prepared by the purchase department in consultation with production department.

(iv) There should be proper classification and coding of each material for effective control.

(v) In order to maintain optimum level of inventory in store, it is essential that various stock levels like maximum, minimum, re-ordering and danger levels for each type of materials should be fixed by the purchase department.

(vi) An efficient system of internal control should be in operation so that all the transactions related to inventory are automatically checked and properly recorded.

(vii) There should be an efficient stock control procedure in operation in store. The verification of stock maintained in the stores should be a regular practice so that any discrepancy could be identified and remedial measures could be taken to avoid such recurrence.

(viii) There should be proper accounting of inventory so that accurate cost of inventory could be assigned to the product.

(ix) The management should always keep a watchful eye on all activities related to inventory management through the evaluation of reports submitted to him regularly.

5.5 INVENTORY CONTROL TECHNIQUES

A proper inventory control system helps in reducing the cost of inventory thereby the cost of production. This will increase the profits and ease the liquidity problem of the organisation. The following are the important techniques of inventory control which are used by the organisations depending upon their nature and activities:

5.5.1 Determination of Stock Levels

In order to maintain the optimum level of inventory in stores, it is essential to set different levels of each material put in stores. This technique helps in purchasing of materials as well as avoiding over or understocking of materials in stores. It is the responsibility of the storekeeper to follow these levels strictly. These stock levels are:

1. **Maximum Level:** The maximum level indicates the maximum quantity of an item of material which can be held in stock at any time. Therefore, the stock of material should not exceed this level any time otherwise it will lead to overstocking. It can be expressed with help of the following formula:

   Maximum Level = Re-ordering Level + Re-ordering Quantity
   – (Minimum Consumption × Minimum Re-order Period)

   In deciding the maximum level a number of factors are taken into considerations which serve as a guide. These factors may be:

   (a) Maximum requirement at any point of time.
   (b) Availability of storage space.
   (c) Storage costs.
   (d) Availability of funds.
   (e) Rate of consumption of materials.
   (f) Replenishment period.
   (g) Extent of price fluctuations.
   (h) Material loss possibilities due to nature of material like evaporation, pilferage, absorbing moisture etc.
   (i) Seasonal nature of supply of materials.
   (j) Risk of obsolescence due to change in fashion or specifications.

2. **Minimum Level:** Minimum level represents the lowest quantity which must be maintained in hand all times. Therefore, the stock of material should not be less than this level at any time otherwise it will lead to understocking or shortage resulting into stoppage of production process or loss of sale. This can be calculated with the help of the following formula:

   Minimum Level = Re-ordering Level
   – (Normal Consumption × Normal Re-order Period)

   The following factors are to be considered by the purchase officer while deciding this level:

   (a) Nature of material
   (b) Consumption rate during lead time
   (c) Replenishment period

3. **Re-order Level:** When the stock in hand touches this level, it is an indication that action for fresh order of material is to be initiated. Re-

ordering level (ROL) is fixed between the maximum and minimum level. Re-order level is also called Re-order point. Re-order point is that level of inventory which has to be maintained for consumption during lead time. It can be expressed with the help of the following formula:

Re-ordering Level = Maximum Consumption × Maximum Re-order Period

or

= Minimum level + Average rate of consumption × Average time required to get fresh delivery

In order to decide re-order level, the following factors have to be taken into consideration:

(a) Lead time
(b) Consumption during lead time
(c) Maximum usage
(d) Economic order quantity

4. **Danger Level:** It is the level beyond which stock of material should not touch or fall in any case. This level is fixed below the minimum level. When the stock reaches to this level, normal issues of material are stopped and very urgent action is required for the purchase of material. This level can be calculated with the help of the following formula:

   Danger Level = Normal consumption × Maximum re-order period for emergency purchases

   However, the existence of this stock level indicates that a situation of stockout about to arise. This level is generally fixed for those types of materials which are used against more than one order or product.

5. **Average Stock Level:** The average stock level is the average of maximum and minimum level. It is calculated with the help of following formula:

   $$\text{Average Stock Level} = \text{Minimum Stock Level} + \frac{\text{Re-ordering Quantity}}{2}$$

   If the re-order level or re-ordering quantity is not known then the following formula shall be used:

   $$\text{Average Stock Level} = \frac{\text{Maximum Level} + \text{Minimum Level}}{2}$$

ILLUSTRATION 5.1: In a manufacturing company, the consumption of material is as follows:

Maximum consumption	–	24,000 units per week
Maximum Re-ordering period for emergency purchases	–	2 weeks

Minimum consumption	– 8,000 units per week
Normal consumption	– 16,000 units per week
Re-order quantity	– 96,000 units
Minimum lead time	– 4 weeks
Maximum lead time	– 6 weeks

You are required to compute the following stock levels of material from the above information:

(i) Re-order Level (ii) Minimum Level (iii) Maximum Level
(iv) Danger Level (v) Average Level

Solution:

(i) Re-order Level = Maximum Consumption × Maximum Re-order Period

= 24,000 × 6
= 1,44,000 units

(ii) Minimum Level = Re-order Level – (Normal Consumption × Normal Re-order Period)

$$= 1{,}44{,}000 - \left(16{,}000 \times \frac{4+6}{2}\right)$$

= 1,44,000 – 80,000
= 64,000 units

(iii) Maximum Level = Re-order Level + Re-order Quantity – (Minimum Consumption × Minimum Re-order Period)

= 1,44,000 + 96,000 – (8,000 × 4)
= 2,40,000 – 32,000
= 2,08,000 units

(iv) Danger Level = Normal Consumption × Maximum Re-order Period for Emergency Purchases

= 16,000 × 2
= 32,000 units

(v) $\text{Average Level} = \text{Minimum Level} + \dfrac{\text{Re-order Quantity}}{2}$

$$= 64{,}000 + \frac{96{,}000}{2}$$

= 64,000 + 48,000
= 1,12,000 units

ILLUSTRATION 5.2: A manufacturer has submitted the following information regarding the requirement of material:

Month	Budgeted consumption (Units)
January, 2021	1,000
February, 2021	2,000

March, 2021	4,000
April, 2021	5,000
May, 2021	4,000
June, 2021	2,000
Re-order Period	4 to 6 months
Re-order quantity	2,000 units

You are required to calculate:

(a) Re-order Point (b) Minimum Level (c) Maximum Level
(d) Average Stock Level using re-order quantity

Solution:

(a) Re-order Point = Maximum consumption × Maximum re-order period
= 5,000 × 6 = 30,000 units

(b) Minimum Level = Re-order level – (Normal consumption × Normal re-order period)

$$= 30{,}000 - 3{,}000 \times \frac{4+6}{2}$$

= 30,000 – 15,000 = 15,000 units

(c) Maximum Level = Re-order level + Re-order quantity – (Minimum consumption × Minimum re-order period)
= (30,000 + 2,000) – (1,000 × 4)
= 32,000 – 4,000
= 28,000 units

(d) $$\text{Average Stock Level} = \text{Minimum level} + \frac{\text{Re-order quantity}}{2}$$

$$= 15{,}000 + \frac{2{,}000}{2}$$

= 15,000 + 1,000 = 16,000 units

Working Note:

$$\text{Normal Usage} = \frac{\text{Total consumption}}{\text{No. of months}}$$

$$= \frac{1{,}000 + 2{,}000 + 4{,}000 + 5{,}000 + 4{,}000 + 2{,}000}{6}$$

= 3,000 units

5.5.2 Economic Order Quantity

The purpose of inventory control is to maintain optimum level of inventory so that the cost should be minimum. A firm must decide the quantity that should be ordered. The quantity to be purchased should neither be small nor big. The purpose is that the purchase should be economical. The Economic Order

Quantity is to be fixed in such a manner as to minimise the total variable cost of managing inventory. This cost is made up of two parts:

(a) Carrying Costs
(b) Ordering Costs

(a) Carrying Costs: It is the cost of holding and maintaining the materials in stores in a good condition. These costs include:

(i) Financing cost
(ii) Storage space cost
(iii) Wastage and loss of material cost
(iv) Risk of obsolescence and deterioration in quality cost
(v) Handling and transfer cost
(vi) Insurance premium, Rent and Warehousing cost
(vii) Clerical cost
(viii) Storage equipment cost

(b) Ordering Costs: It is the cost of placing an order for the purchase of material and include the following costs:

(i) Cost of placing an order
(ii) Cost of following an order
(iii) Cost of receiving an order
(iv) Cost of inspection
(v) Expenses of purchase department

Thus, both the above costs are conflicting to each other. If the management decides to increase the quantity of purchase, the ordering cost decreases while the carrying cost will increase and vice-versa. A balance is, therefore, to be maintained between these two costs. The Economic Order Quantity (EOQ) is one where the carrying and ordering costs are minimum or equal for a size of the order. This system is also known as fixed order quantity system.

Assumptions underlying EOQ

While calculating the EOQ, the following assumptions are made:

(i) The supply of materials is normal, i.e., orders placed are immediately replenished.
(ii) The prices of the materials are stable and are known.
(iii) The quantity of the items to be consumed during a particular period is known.
(iv) The ordering cost and carrying cost are known and fixed.
(v) No constraints on the size of each lot, i.e., truck capacity, storage space, handling etc.
(vi) Each order is received in a single delivery.

Determination of EOQ

The following information are required for the calculation of EOQ:

(i) Total units to be purchased yearly
(ii) Cost of placing per order
(iii) Annual carrying cost per unit

The following formula is used for the calculation of EOQ:

$$EOQ = \sqrt{\frac{2\,AO}{C}}$$

Where A = Annual consumption in units
O = Cost of placing per order
C = Annual carrying cost per unit

Derivation of EOQ Formula

Let A = Annual Consumption
O = Procurement cost per order
C = Annual carrying cost per unit
Q = Economic order Quantity

Ordering Cost = No. of orders placed in a year × Cost per order

$$= \frac{A}{Q} \times O$$

Carrying Cost = Average Value of inventory in a year × Annual carrying cost per unit

$$= \frac{Q}{2} \times C$$

The total cost will be minimum when
Ordering Cost = Inventory carrying cost

$$\frac{A \times O}{Q} = \frac{Q \times C}{2}$$

$$Q^2C = 2AO$$

$$Q = \sqrt{\frac{2\,AO}{C}}$$

Use of EOQ model to Management

The EOQ recommends that how much to order or what will be order quantity. But it is not essential that economic order quantity will be ordered every time. The final decision regarding order quantity lies in the hands of management depending upon the various conditions like inventory on hand, supplier's acceptance for quantity, discount offers, funds availability etc. The management has to exercise his judgement in deciding how much to order (EOQ) and when to order (ROL or ROP). The management may modify the final order quantity as suggested by EOQ model. Following options may be before the management for consideration while taking decision for final order quantity:

(i) Final order quantity may be more than EOQ if the supplier offers any discount in price of material.
(ii) Final order quantity may be less than EOQ if the inventory in hand is at reasonable level.
(iii) Ordering quantity which will result in whole number of orders per year.
(iv) Ordering quantity may be modified on account of quantity to be supplied accepted by the supplier.

ILLUSTRATION 5.3: The cost accounting records of a manufacturing concern provide the following data:

		₹
(i)	Purchase department staff salaries	2,60,000
(ii)	Stores staff salaries	1,60,000
(iii)	Cost of security of warehouse	60,000
(iv)	Cost of placing order	30,000
(v)	Cost of follow-up of orders	20,000
(vi)	Warehouse insurance	40,000
(vii)	Cost of inward inspection	30,000
(viii)	Cost of materials handling	50,000
(ix)	Cost of obsolescence and materials wastage	20,000
(x)	Storage equipment cost	40,000

The firm has an average inventory of ₹ 37 lakh and has placed 3,400 orders in a year. You are required to calculate cost per order and inventory carrying cost as percentage.

Solution:

Calculation of Ordering Cost:	₹
Purchase department staff salaries	2,60,000
Cost of placing order	30,000
Cost of follow-up of orders	20,000
Cost of inward inspection	30,000
Total Ordering Cost	3,40,000

$$\text{Ordering Cost per Order} = \frac{3,40,000}{3,400} = ₹\ 100$$

Calculation of Carrying Cost:	₹
Stores staff salaries	1,60,000
Cost of security of warehouse	60,000

Warehouse insurance	40,000
Cost of materials handling	50,000
Cost of obsolescence and materials wastage	20,000
Storage equipment cost	40,000
Total Carrying Cost	3,70,000

$$\text{Inventory Carrying Cost} = \frac{3,70,000}{37,00,000} \times 100 = 10\%$$

ILLUSTRATION 5.4: An auto company purchases a spare part at the rate of ₹ 2 per unit. The annual consumption is 18,000 units. The ordering cost is ₹ 200 and carrying cost is 10% per year of the average inventory. You are required to calculate:

(i) EOQ
(ii) No. of orders in a year
(iii) If the company gets 10% discount in placing single order, should the company accept the order.
(iv) Find break even discount percentage which matches EOQ ordering.

Solution:

(i) $\text{EOQ} = \sqrt{\frac{2AO}{C}} = \sqrt{\frac{2 \times 18,000 \times 200}{.20}} = 6,000 \text{ units}$

(ii) $\text{No. of Orders in a year} = \frac{18,000}{6,000} = 3 \text{ orders}$

(iii) Evaluation of Discount Proposal:

(a) Total Cost at EOQ:

Spare parts cost	18000 × 2	₹	36,000
Ordering cost	3 × 200	₹	600
Carrying cost	$\frac{6,000}{2} \times .20$	₹	600
Total cost		₹	37,200

(b) Total cost at single order, i.e., 18,000 units:

Spare parts cost	18000 × 1.80	₹	32,400
Ordering Cost	1 × 200	₹	200
Carrying Cost	$\frac{18,000}{2} \times .18$	₹	1,620
Total Cost		₹	34,220

Decision:

Since the total cost at discount offer is less than to total cost at EOQ, the company is to accept the discount offer of 10% on unit price.

(iv) Determination of Break-even discount percentage which matches EOQ ordering:

Let Y be the new discount price to match EOQ ordering
Annual consumption (A) = 18,000 units
Ordering quantity to avail discount (Q) = 18,000 units
Ordering Cost (O) = ₹ 200 per order
Carrying Cost (C) = ₹ 0.20
Total Cost at Break-even discount (TC BE/Disc.)

$$= AY + \frac{A}{Q} \times O + \frac{Q}{2} \times CY$$

$$= 18,000\ Y + \frac{18,000}{18,000} \times 200 + \frac{18,000}{2} \times 0.20\ Y$$

= 18,000 Y + 200 + 1,800 Y
= 19,800 Y + 200
TC BE/Disc. = TC EOQ
19,800 Y + 200 = 37,200
19,800 Y = 37,200 – 200
19,800 Y = 37,000

$$Y = \frac{37,000}{19,800} = 1.868$$

$$\text{Break-even \% discount} = \frac{P - Y}{P} \times 100$$

$$= \frac{2 - 1,868}{2} \times 100$$

= 6.6%

5.5.3 ABC Analysis

This concept is based on the selective inventory management. In large organisations, different categories of materials are kept in the store. In order to exercise proper control on stores, it is essential that the stored items should be classified according to their value so that the most valuable items may be paid more attention regarding safety and care as compared to other items of materials in stores. Thus, ABC method is used to exercise effective control over the inventory on the basis of their value. This is also called Control by Importance and Exception (CIE). Under this method, the stores are divided into three classes known as A, B and C. The items of high value but less in percentage of total items handled are put under 'A' category. The items relatively less important and equal or moderate in value and equal in percentage of total items are put under 'B' category. The rest items which are of least importance and low in value and higher percentage in total items are put in 'C' category. Thus, the purpose of ABC analysis is to develop policy guidelines for effective control system for inventories classified under ABC category.

Example 5.1:

The ABC analysis has been explained with the help of the following example:

Class	*No. of items*	*% of total No. of items*	*Value ₹*	*% of total value*
A	100	10	70,000	70
B	200	20	20,000	20
C	700	70	10,000	10
	1,000	100	1,00,000	100

In the above example 5.1 'A' items represent 70% of the total investment but only 10% of the total number of items. Therefore, a strict control must be applied on these items in estimating requirements, fixing stock levels, estimating lead time, placing in store, housing equipment etc. Group 'B' category items are next in importance having moderate in value requires no such control as in case of items 'A'. Similarly, the items under 'C' category comprising 70% in total number of items and 10% only in value need only a simple and inexpensive system of control. In other words, routine control may be exercised. Example 5.1 has also been exhibited with the help of following Figure:

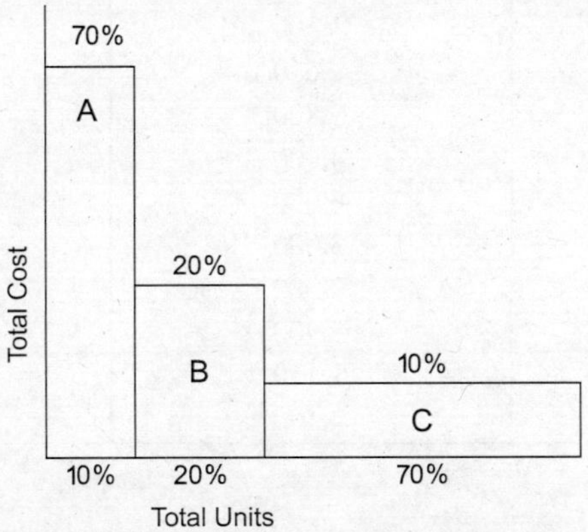

Treatment of ABC classes of inventory or order of control

S. No.	*Basis*	*A Category*	*B Category*	*C Category*
1.	Control	Strict	Moderate	Low
2.	Requirements	Exact	Near to requirement	Estimated
3.	Placing of material	Individual	Individual	Group
4.	Checking	Continuous and close	Occasionally and moderate	On and off

(Contd.)

S. No.	*Basis*	*A Category*	*B Category*	*C Category*
5.	Safety stock	No or very low	Low	Large
6.	Handling	Senior officers	Middle management	Lower staff
7.	Replenishment	Regular	Periodic	As per need
8.	Lead time	Maximum efforts to reduce lead time	Moderate efforts to reduce lead time	Minimum efforts to reduce lead time
9.	Review	Fortnightly review	Bimonthly review	Half yearly review
10.	Control statements	Weekly	Monthly	Quarterly

ILLUSTRATION 5.5: Chitaranjan Industries is considering a selective control for its inventories. From the following data, draw a plan of ABC selective control for presentation to the management:

Items	*Annual usage (Units)*	*Unit cost* (₹)
1.	800	60.00
2.	2,400	1.00
3.	1,500	10.00
4.	610	122.00
5.	3,800	1.00
6.	4,000	0.50
7.	6,000	0.21
8.	3,000	3.50
9.	300	100.00
10.	2,900	0.40
11.	1,150	10.00
12.	4,100	3.00

Solution:

Ranking of Items as per value

Items	*Annual usage (Units)*	*Unit cost* (₹)	*Annual usage value* (₹)	*Ranking*
1.	800	60.00	48,000	II
2.	2,400	1.00	2,400	IX
3.	1,500	10.00	15,000	IV
4.	610	122.00	74,420	I
5.	3,800	1.00	3,800	VIII
6.	4,000	0.50	2,000	X
7.	6,000	0.21	1,260	XI
8.	3,000	3.50	10,500	VII

(Contd.)

Items	*Annual usage (Units)*	*Unit cost (₹)*	*Annual usage value (₹)*	*Ranking*
9.	300	100.00	30,000	III
10.	2,900	0.40	1,160	XII
11.	1,150	10.00	11,500	VI
12.	4,100	3.00	12,300	V
TOTAL			**2,12,340**	

Statement of ABC Analysis

Items	*Rank*	*Annual usage (₹)*	*Class*	*Annual usage value in each class*	*% of total items in each class*	*% of total annual usage value in each class*
4.	I	74,420				
1.	II	48,000	A	1,52,420	25	71.78
9.	III	30,000				
3.	IV	15,000				
12.	V	12,300	B	49,300	33.33	23.22
11.	VI	11,500				
8.	VII	10,500				
5.	VIII	3,800				
2.	IX	2,400				
6.	X	2,000	C	10,620	41.67	5
7.	XI	1,260				
10.	XII	1,160				
		2,12,340		2,12,340	100.00	100.00

The above table shows that 71.78% of the total investment in inventory is having 25% share in total items. Therefore, it is categorized under 'A' and strict control is necessary of these items. Similarly, 23.22% of the total investment in inventory is 33.33% of the total items which constitute under List 'B'. In this case moderate control on these items can be exercised. The remaining items 41.67% having the 5% investment in inventory are put under category 'C'. Since, the value is low, less emphasis may be given on these items.

Advantages of ABC Analysis

The analysis has the following advantages:

(i) A strict control is exercised according to the value of materials. Hence, material losses can be minimised.

(ii) Investment in materials is made according to their importance, value and use. Thus, funds are released for more profitable investment.

(iii) Storage costs are minimised as only required quantity of materials are purchased.

(iv) Inventory control cost is reduced due to different degree of control are exercised according to the value of items. For example, no need to exercise regular control for 'C' group items.

(v) Quick purchase of materials avoids stoppage of production and minimises cost of placing order and also follow-up cost.

Limitations of ABC Analysis

The following are the limitations of the analysis:

(i) It is not essential that low monetary value items of inventory are not vital or having no importance for running of production process smoothly. Some times low value item, i.e., nut or bolt becomes vital for the maintenance of the machine.

(ii) Importance given according to value is not true in every circumstances.

(iii) Since the prices of materials keep on changing, therefore, ABC analysis should be reviewed from time to time so that classification of materials could be revised accordingly.

5.5.4 Perpetual Inventory System

It is the objective of purchase department to know the stock position of every item of material in the stores from time to time. Therefore, it is necessary to draw the balance of the material after every receipt and issue. This system facilitates continuous stock checking and avoids closing down the firm for stock taking. Perpetual inventory means system of stock records maintained by the cost accounting department and continuous stock taking. The **ICMA** defines perpetual inventory system as "a system of records maintained by the controlling department which reflects physical movement of stock and their current balance" Thus, the perpetual inventory system consists of two elements:

1. **System of Stock Records:** It is the system of recording every receipt and issue so as to determine stock in hand at any time in quantity or value or both without the need of physical count of stock. The two stock records are maintained one by the storekeeper known as Bin Card, i.e., quantitative perpetual inventory and second by the cost accounting department known as Stores Ledger, i.e., quantitative cum value perpetual inventory. The records are maintained for each type of materials. The purpose of these records is that the balance shown in Bin Card should correspond with the balance shown in Stores Ledger on a particular date and a frequent checking of these two records must be made on regular basis. If there is any difference in the balances shown by these two records, the matter must be further examined.
2. **Continuous Stock Taking:** The perpetual inventory system is not complete without a systematic procedure for physical verification of stores. The continuous stock taking means the comparison of stock

records with the actual quantity of material in stock by physical counting. This ensures the accuracy of perpetual inventory records, i.e., Bin Card and Stores Ledger. The process of stock verification is carried out throughout the year by a trained staff.

Difference in Stock Balance

It is possible that the balance of stock shown by the Bin Card and Stores Ledger may differ as well as this may also differ from the actual balance of stock as ascertained by physical verification. The difference in stock balance may arise mainly due to the following reasons which can be avoided and cannot be avoided:

(i) **Avoidable causes:** The difference in the stock balance on account of the following reasons can be avoided:

(a) Clerical mistakes, e.g., wrong posting and casting, no posting.
(b) Pilferage and theft.
(c) Carelessness in material handling and putting in wrong Bin.
(d) Short or over issue of materials.

(ii) **Unavoidable causes:** The unavoidable causes may be:

(a) Loss of material due to shrinkage and evaporation.
(b) Absorption of moistures.
(c) Due to fire, riots etc.
(d) Due to breaking of bulk materials into small pieces.

The above unavoidable causes can be checked to some extent by taking extra care and using of proper housing equipment for materials.

Rectification of Discrepancies

The discrepancies detected during the physical verification of stock may be of two types either excess balance or short balance. Excess balance of stock is more than the recorded balance in Bin Card and Stores Ledger and vice-versa. Thus, the causes of discrepancies must be explained and remedial measures should be taken for avoiding such discrepancies in future and corrected entries should be made accordingly in the books.

Advantages

Perpetual inventory system is essential for material control. The advantages are:

(i) Records are maintained properly due to continuous stock taking.
(ii) The data of the stock positions are readily available to the purchase department.
(iii) Discrepancies are easily located and rectified in time to avoid their recurrence.

(iv) Continuous stock taking acts as a moral check on the storekeeper and his staff.

(v) It ensures prompt availability of stock balance for the preparation of final accounts.

(vi) A systematic review of the perpetual inventory system identifies the existence of surplus, obsolete and slow-moving materials.

(vii) Errors and shortage or excess of stock are readily discovered.

(viii) A system of internal checks remains in operation due to preparation and reconciling the Bin Card and Stores Ledger from time to time.

(ix) The stock verification can be done without temporarily shutting the factory.

(x) Investments in materials in stores can be made within the prescribed limits or control.

Limitations

Perpetual inventory system has some limitations which are:

(i) The work of continuous stock taking depends upon the up-to-date preparation of Bin Card and Stores Ledger. In the absence of it effective control cannot be exercised.

(ii) Continuous stock checking makes an impression on the storekeeper and his staff of their error findings exercise.

(iii) It is expensive in case of less items in stock.

5.5.5 Just-in-Time (JIT) System

Inventory involves two types of costs, i.e., ordering cost and carrying or holding cost. JIT system takes into account enormous carrying cost. Now-a-days organisations are interested in producing customised products. They do not want to make investment in different kinds of materials and incur carrying cost in stores and warehouse. Thus, they want to gain from smaller purchasing, i.e., customised purchasing of materials and save funds for some other productive purposes. The smaller and more frequent purchase order is called just-in-time purchasing. This technique ensures flow of material to the production as and when required in needed quantity and quality. JIT moves outside the assumption of EOQ. This system is also called KANBAN system of inventory control. The system takes into account elimination of all wastes in storing and carrying the materials and also in production process. This is possible by providing right material, right place and at the right time by making frequent purchase order.

Characteristics of JIT System

The salient features of JIT system are:

(i) Pull method of material inflow to the production process is used by purchasing of material in such way that delivery is assured before their demand to the production process.

(ii) The system constantly provides good quality of material to production by frequent fresh orders instead of supplying from stores.

(iii) The small lot sizes of materials are purchased thereby avoiding of locking of funds in inventory unnecessarily.

(iv) The frequent purchase of materials develops good relation with the supplier.

Objectives of JIT System

The objectives of JIT system are:

(i) Assures a continuous and rapid flow of material.

(ii) Provide right quality of material at right place and right time.

(iii) Produce customised products, i.e., according to the specification and demand of customer.

(iv) Ensures delivery of the product on time.

(v) Produce products with perfect quality and zero defects.

(vi) Ensure zero waste policy in terms of materials, labour and equipment.

(vii) The system supports zero inventory level while producing products.

(viii) Avoids overproduction just to avoid delays.

(ix) Eliminates non-value-added activities.

(x) Ensures zero breakdown policy.

(xi) Avoids unnecessary stock of inventory, i.e., raw materials, work-in-process and finished goods.

Essentials of JIT Purchasing

In order to implement JIT purchasing effectively, the essentials are:

(i) Preparation of the list of possible materials used in the production.

(ii) Prepare the list of prospective suppliers located near the buying firm.

(iii) Develop the close tie-up with the supplier.

(iv) Develop long-term relationship with few suppliers.

(v) Suppliers should be reliable that means they could supply required quantity and quality and adhere delivery schedules.

Benefits of JIT System

The following are the benefits available to the firm and the customers with the application of the system:

(i) On account of zero inventory policy, there is no need of keeping inventory in stock and thereby inventory levels are reduced significantly and also locking of funds in inventory.

(ii) Due to standardised production process, processing time can be reduced.

(iii) Ensure good quality product by using good quality of material and minimising scrap.

(iv) Reduced customer related problems by producing and supplying customised products.

(v) Due to good relations with the supplier replenishment time of material can be reduced.

(vi) Investment in inventory is reduced due to low or no level of inventory in stock.

(vii) Carrying costs are reduced.

(viii) Reduction in office paper work in purchasing, storing, issue of materials etc.

(ix) Frequent purchase of material keeps the price of material realistic or near to market price.

(x) Reduction in warehouse cost due to immediate delivery of the product or keeping minimum stock of finished goods.

Limitations of JIT System

The limitations of JIT system are:

(i) The system pre-supposes the good relations among suppliers, workers and management.

(ii) It is not essential that all the time supply of good quality material at right time and right place can be maintained.

(iii) Ordering cost will increase by frequent purchasing of materials.

(iv) There are always chances of increase in price of materials due to small lot purchasing.

(v) The suppliers may dictate their terms and conditions later on.

(vi) There are chances of non-availability of good quality of materials from local supplier.

(vii) It may not be possible to get supply from suppliers as and when needed in required quality and quantity.

5.5.6 Control Ratios

Inventory control may also be managed by the use of different inventory control ratios. These ratios may be:

Input-Output Ratio

This ratio helps in exercising effective control over the usage of material (input) in manufacturing of finished products. It is the ratio of input quantity of material and quantity of material in the output (finished product). It can be expressed as:

$$\text{Input-Output Ratio} = \frac{\text{Input Quantity of Material}}{\text{Quantity of Material in Output}} \times 100$$

The ratio is helpful in controlling wastages in production process and knowing whether input-output ratio is favourable or unfavourable. The cost of material in the finished product can be ascertained by multiplying cost per unit of material by input-output ratio.

ILLUSTRATION 5.6: From the following information, calculate the input-output ratio and material cost of finished output:

Input material	600 kg
Cost per unit	₹ 12
Output	500 kg

Solution:

$$\text{Input-output Ratio} = \frac{600}{500} \times 100$$

$$= 120\%$$

$$\text{Material cost of finished output} = 12 \times \frac{120}{100}$$

$$= ₹\ 14.40$$

Inventory Turnover Ratio

Inventory turnover ratio indicates a firm's efficiency of inventory management. It shows the velocity of the movement of inventory, i.e., slow, moderate or fast. Inventory ratios may be calculated for finished goods and raw materials separately.

For Finished Goods

The ratio shows the speed with which the finished goods inventory converted into sales or revenue. The higher the ratio, better it is which indicates that inventories selling quickly. On the contrary, a low inventory turnover ratio means finished goods are lying in the godown idle for long time or over investment in inventory. This may result into blocking of funds, chances of becoming obsolete or out of fashion, dull business etc. In such situation, the management has to take immediate action to convert it into sales by adopting suitable promotional measures. It may be expressed with the help of the following formula:

$$\text{Inventory Turnover Ratio} = \frac{\text{Net sales/Cost of Goods Sold}}{\text{Average Inventory}}$$

If cost of goods sold is not known, the inventory turnover ratio may be calculated with the help of net sales.

Inventory conversion period indicates the age of inventory. It implies that in how much time on an average the inventory will be converted into sales. If the conversion period is high, it shows the excessive blockage of funds with inventory and increase in the chances of becoming obsolete. It also shows the inefficiency of marketing/sales department and negligence on the part of the management. It may be calculated with the help of the following formula:

$$\text{Inventory Conversion Period} = \frac{\text{No. of Days in a Year}}{\text{Inventory Turnover Ratio}}$$

ILLUSTRATION 5.7: The following information have been obtained from the records of Shantanu Ltd.:

	₹
Credit sales	3,00,000
Cash sales	1,20,000
Return inward	20,000
Opening inventory	45,000
Closing inventory	55,000
Gross profit ratio is 25%	

Compute:

(i) Inventory Turnover Ratio
(ii) Inventory Conversion Period

Solution:

Net Sales = 3,00,000 + 1,20,000 – 20,000 = ₹ 4,00,000

Gross Profit = 4,00,000 × 25% = ₹ 1,00,000

Cost of Goods Sold = 4,00,000 – 1,00,000 = ₹ 3,00,000

$$\text{Average Inventory} = \frac{45{,}000 + 55{,}000}{2} = ₹\ 50{,}000$$

(i) $$\text{Inventory Turnover Ratio} = \frac{\text{Cost of Goods Sold}}{\text{Average Inventory}}$$

$$= \frac{3{,}00{,}000}{50{,}000} = 6 \text{ times}$$

(ii) $$\text{Inventory Conversion Period} = \frac{\text{No. of Days in a Year}}{\text{Inventory Turnover Ratio}}$$

$$= \frac{365}{6} = 60.82 \text{ or } 61 \text{ days.}$$

For Raw Material

Inventory turnover ratio may also be calculated for raw material. It is the ratio of cost of material consumed to the average stock of raw material during the period. The ratio shows the number of times inventory (raw material) consumed and replenished. Similarly, raw material conversion period may also be measured by dividing number of days in a year or period by raw material turnover ratio. The ratio indicates the movement of raw material is slow, moderate or fast and dormant and obsolete. With the help of this ratio, management can take decision for replenishment of material as well as remedial measures for slow moving, dormant and obsolete materials. The following formulae shall be used for calculating these ratios:

$$\text{Raw Material Turnover Ratio} = \frac{\text{Cost of Material Consumed}}{\text{Average Stock of Material}}$$

$$\text{Raw Material Conversion Period} = \frac{\text{No. of Days in a Year/Period}}{\text{Raw Material Turnover Ratio}}$$

ILLUSTRATION 5.8: The following information are available from the Bin Card of raw material 'X' of which Code No. is 201:

Stock on 1st January, 2021	₹ 20,000
Stock on 31st December, 2021	₹ 10,000
Purchases during the year	₹ 65,000

Calculate:

(i) Raw Material 'X' Turnover Ratio
(ii) Raw Material 'X' Conversion Period

Solution:

Calculation of material consumed:

	₹
Opening stock	20,000
Add: Purchases	65,000
	85,000
Less: Closing stock	10,000
Material consumed	75,000

(i) $$\text{Raw Material 'X' Turnover Ratio} = \frac{\text{Raw Material Consumed}}{\text{Average Stock}}$$

$$= \frac{75,000}{15,000} = 5 \text{ times}$$

(ii) $$\text{Raw Material 'X' Conversion Period} = \frac{\text{No. of Days in a Year}}{\text{Raw Material Turnover Ratio}}$$

$$= \frac{365}{5} = 73 \text{ days}$$

It means that the stock of raw material 'X' is held for more than two months or 73 days.

5.6 SELECTIVE TECHNIQUES OF INVENTORY CONTROL

The following techniques may be used as per the requirement and nature of the material:

5.6.1 VED Analysis

This method of inventory control has been designed for controlling the spare parts and ensuring its supply to the production process. The demand for spare parts largely depends upon the maintenance of plant and machinery. Though, these parts are low in value but the absence of it can stop the function of plant and machinery. Its full name is Vital, Essential and Desirable Analysis. In this analysis the spare parts are classified under three categories as the name indicates:

(i) **Vital (V):** The vital spare parts are those without which production process cannot run smoothly. The absence of these spare parts may lead to stoppage of production process. These must be adequately stored and stockout of such spare parts is not allowed in any case.

(ii) **Essential (E):** These spare parts are essential for the smooth running of production. The absence of these parts in store will not lead to the stoppage of production process immediately. The non-availability of each spare part can be tolerated for few hours or maximum a day. Therefore, stock of these spare parts may be kept low.

(iii) **Desirable (D):** The desirable spares are those which are necessary but the non-availability of these parts will not lead to immediately stoppage of production. The absence of these parts for a few days or maximum a week can be tolerated. Therefore, the stock of these parts may be kept very low or in case of requirement, it may be arranged from the market.

5.6.2 FSN Analysis

This analysis is based on the consumption pattern of inventory. In this analysis, consumption pattern of inventories is classified into three categories, i.e., Fast moving (F), Slow moving (S) and Non-moving (N). Fast moving materials are those which are consumed in production process regularly. It may also be called main material used in the production of the product. Therefore, proper attention has to be given by the management for the availability of such material all the time. On the other hand, slow moving materials are consumed less frequently. Hence, the stock of such materials should be maintained at minimum level. A careful attention is needed in respect of non-moving stock which may become dormant or obsolete.

5.6.3 HML Analysis

This analysis is similar to the ABC Analysis. The difference is that under ABC Analysis materials are classified on the basis of total usage value while in HML Analysis materials are classified on the basis of unit cost. The inventories are classified in the HML analysis as High (H), Medium (M) and Low (L) unit cost. Under this analysis, inventories belonging to H category are given utmost importance and strict control is exercised while in M category inventory items moderate control is exercised. The inventory items belong to L category are given least degree of control due to low unit cost.

5.6.4 SDE Analysis

According to this analysis, materials are classified on the basis of their availability. The material items are classified into three categories viz. Scarce (S), Difficult (D) and Easy (E). The scarce items mean which are in short supply and therefore, stock of such items should be maintained more than the requirement irrespective of their value to avoid stoppage of production process. In case of D items, the materials are available but cannot procured easily. Therefore, constant efforts are to be made in obtaining such items. E items are easily available in the market. Therefore, no extra efforts are required in procurement of such items.

5.6.5 SOS Analysis

Under this technique of inventory control, materials are classified under two categories: (a) seasonal items and (b) off-season items. This analysis helps in implementing a proper strategy of material purchase. Seasonal items should be given more importance while purchasing.

5.6.6 GOLF Analysis

According to this analysis, G stands for government supply, O stands for open supply, L stands for local supplies and F stands for foreign supplies. A proper care has to be given to government and foreign supplies because it requires to observe certain rules and regulations and paper work for procurement of items of materials. In case of open and local supplies, there is no problem in procurement.

THEORETICAL QUESTIONS

I. Short Answer Type Questions

1. Define inventory Control.
2. What are financial objectives of inventory control?

3. Explain essentials of inventory control.
4. What is the importance of inventory control?
5. Define Maximum level of stock.
6. Explain Re-order level.
7. What is Danger level?
8. What is Carrying cost?
9. Explain EOQ.
10. Explain Perpetual Inventory System.
11. Define Input-Output Ratio.
12. Explain JIT System.
13. Explain VED Analysis.
14. What is FSN Analysis?
15. Explain HML Analysis.

II. Long Answer Type Questions

1. Define inventory control. Explain objectives of inventory control.
2. Describe the importance and essentials of inventory control.
3. What is Economic Order Quantity? How is it fixed? Explain.
4. What is meant by maximum level, minimum level and re-order level? What are the factors that governs the fixing of these levels? Explain.
5. Define Perpetual Inventory System. Explain its advantages and limitations.
6. What is ABC analysis? How is it useful as a tool of inventory control? Explain.
7. Describe the selective inventory control techniques.
8. Discuss the utility of the following as inventory control techniques:
   (i) ABC Analysis
   (ii) Economic Order Quantity
   (iii) Perpetual Inventory System
9. Write a note on JIT System.
10. Write notes on:
    (i) VED Analysis
    (ii) FSN Analysis
    (iii) SDE Analysis

III. Numerical Questions

1. In a manufacturing company a material is used as follows:

(a) Normal usage	600 units per week
(b) Maximum usage	840 units per week
(c) Minimum usage	480 units per week
(d) Re-ordering quantity	7200 units
(e) Normal Re-ordering period	12 weeks
(f) Re-ordering period	10 to 15 weeks

Calculate:

(i) Maximum Stock Level (ii) Minimum Stock Level
(iii) Re-order Level (iv) Average Stock Level

Ans: (i) 15000 units, (ii) 5400 units, (iii) 12600 units, and (iv) 9000 units

2. In manufacturing a commodity two components Zinc and Copper are used as follows:

(i)	Normal Consumption	20 units per week each
(ii)	Maximum Consumption	30 units per week each
(iii)	Minimum Consumption	10 units per week each
(iv)	Re-ordering quantity:	
	Zinc	150 units
	Copper	200 units
(v)	Re-ordering period:	
	Zinc	4 to 6 weeks
	Copper	2 to 4 weeks

Compute the following:

(a) Re-order Limit (b) Minimum Limit
(c) Maximum Limit (d) Average Stock

Ans: (a) Zinc-180 units, Copper-120 units; (b) Zinc-80 units, Copper-60 units; (c) Zinc-290 units, Copper-300 units; (d) Zinc-155 units Copper-160 units

3. Material A is used as follows:

Minimum Usage	500 Units per week
Maximum Usage	1500 Units per week
Normal Usage	1000 Units per week
Ordering Quantities	1600 Units
Delivery Period	4 – 6 Weeks

Calculate:

(i) Maximum Level
(ii) Minimum Level
(iii) Ordering Level

(C.A. Inter June, 2009 Executive Program)

Ans: **(i)** Maximum Level-8600 Units, (ii) Minimum Level-4000 Units, and (iii) Ordering Level-9000 Units

4. The following information is available in respect of a component which is used in the manufacturing of the product:

(i)	Maximum Consumption	12000 units per week
(ii)	Maximum Re-order period for emergency purchase	2 weeks
(iii)	Minimum Consumption	4000 units per week
(iv)	Normal Consumption	8000 units per week

(v) Re-order quantity — 48000 units
(vi) Time required for delivery — 4 to 6 weeks

You are required to calculate:

(a) Re-order Level
(b) Minimum Level
(c) Maximum Level
(d) Danger Level
(e) Average Stock Level

Ans: (a) 72,000 units, (b) 32,000 units, (c) 1,04,000 units, (d) 16,000 units, (e) 56,000 units

5. A company uses three raw materials X, Y and Z for the production of its one of the products in respect of which the following information are available:

Raw Materials	*Usage per unit of product*	*Re-order quantity (kg)*	*Price per kg (₹)*	*Delivery Period (weeks)*	*Order Level (kg)*
X	10	10,000	1.00	2 to 4	10,000
Y	4	5,000	3.00	3 to 6	4,000
Z	6	10,000	1.50	2 to 4	

Weekly production varies from 175 to 225 units, averaging 200 units. Compute the following:

(a) Minimum Stock Level of X
(b) Maximum Stock Level of Y
(c) Re-order level of Z
(d) Average Stock Level of X

Ans: (a) 4,000 kg, (b) 6,900 kg, (c) 5,400 kg, (d) 9,000 kg

6. The following information is related to Material X:

Maximum consumption	600 units per month
Minimum consumption	100 units per month
Normal consumption	300 units per month
Yearly consumption	3,600 units
Storage cost	50% of stock value
Ordering cost	₹ 400 per order
Price of material	₹ 64 per unit

Find out:

(i) Re-order Level
(ii) Minimum Stock Level
(iii) Maximum Stock Level
(iv) Average Stock Lavel

(B.Com. D.U.)

Ans: (i) 1200 units, (ii) 750 units, (iii) 1400 units, and (iv) 1075 units

7. ZEE is a product manufactured out of three raw materials M, N and Q. Each unit of ZEE requires 10kg, 8kg and 6 kg of M, N, and Q respectively. The re-order levels of M and N are 15,000 kg and 10,000 kg respectively, while the minimum level of Q is 2,500 kg

The weekly production of ZEE varies from 300 to 500 units, while the weekly average production is 400 units.

You are required to compute:

(i) The minimum stock level of M
(ii) The maximum stock level of N, and
(iii) The re-order level of Q

The following additional data are given:

	M	N	Q
Re-order quantity (in kg)	20,000	15,000	20,000
Delivery (in weeks):			
Minimum	2	4	3
Average	3	5	4
Maximum	4	6	5

(B.Com. D.U.)

Ans: Minimum Stock Level of M 3,000 kg, Maximum Stock Level of N 15,400 kg, ROL of Q 15,000 kg

8. A company consumes 10000 kg of raw material per annum for the production of a product. The cost of raw material is ₹ 2 per kg, and ordering cost is ₹ 50. Storage and carrying cost as a percentage of average inventory is 8%. Number of days in a year is 360. Determine:

   (i) Economic order quantity
   (ii) Number of orders per annum
   (iii) Time between two consecutive orders.

   Ans: (i) 2500 kg, (ii) 4 orders per year, and (iii) 90 days

9. A Company manufactures a special product which requires a component 'Alpha'. The following particulars are collected for the year 2008:

(i)	Annual demand of Alpha	8000 units
(ii)	Cost of placing order	200 per order
(iii)	Cost per unit of Alpha	₹ 400
(iv)	Carrying cost % p.a.	20%

   The Company has been offered a quantity discount of 4% on the purchase of Alpha, provided the order size is 4000 components at a time.

   Required:

   (i) Compute the economic order quantity.
   (ii) Advise whether the quantity discount offer can be accepted.

   (C.A. PE-II, Nov., 2007)

   Ans: (i) EOQ-200 units, Inventory cost per annum at EOQ-₹ 32,16,000 and Inventory cost p.a. with quantity discount ₹ 32,26,000, (ii) Offer should not be accepted

10. Economic enterprise requires 5000 units of a certain item annually. The cost per unit is ₹ 20 and ordering cost per order is ₹ 50. The storage and carrying cost is 10% per year. Calculate:
    (i) Economic order quantity
    (ii) Number of orders per annum
    (iii) What should the firm do if the supplier offers discount as below:

	Order Quantity (Units)	*Discount*
(a)	500	No Discount
(b)	1000–2499	2%
(c)	2500 and above	3%

Ans: (i) 500 units, (ii) 10 orders, (iii) 2% discount offer be accepted

11. A Company manufactures a product from a raw material, which is purchased at ₹ 80 per kg. The Company incurs a handling cost of ₹ 370 plus freight of ₹ 380 per order. The incremental carrying cost of inventory of raw material is ₹ 0.25 per kg per month. In addition, the cost of working capital finance on the investment in inventory of raw material is ₹ 12 per kg per annum. The annual production of the product is 100000 units and 2.5 units are obtained from 1 kg of raw material.

    Required:
    (i) Calculate the economic order quantity of raw material.
    (ii) Advise, how frequently Company should order for procurement be placed.
    (iii) If the Company proposes to rationalised placement of orders on quarterly basis, what percentage of discount in the price of raw material should be negotiated.

    Assume 360 days in a year.

(C.A. Inter, May, 2014)

Ans: EOQ-2000 kg, No. of orders p.a.-200 orders, Frequency of placing orders-18 days, Discount to be negotiated-1.5%

12. A factory buys and uses a component for production at ₹ 10 per unit. Annual requirement is 2,000 units. Carrying cost of inventory is 10% per annum and ordering cost is ₹ 40 per order. The purchase manager argues that the ordering cost is very high, so it is advantageous to place a single order for the entire annual requirement. A discount of 3% is also available if 2,000 units are ordered at a time. Calculate Economic Order Quantity and evaluate the proposal and make recommendations.

(B.Com. D.U.)

Ans: EOQ 400 units, Total cost at EOQ ₹ 20,400 and at 3% discount ₹ 20410. Buying in EOQ is recommended

13. Rajwardhan Industries is considering a selective control for its inventories. From the following data, draw a plan of ABC selective control for presentation to management:

Items	*Units*	*Unit Cost* (₹)
AB	8,000	4.50
CD	24,000	3.00
EF	1,500	10.00
GH	610	22.00
IJ	38,000	1.50
KL	40,000	0.50
MN	60,000	0.21
OP	3,000	3.50
QR	300	9.00
ST	29,000	0.40
UV	11,500	7.20
WX	4,100	6.00

(M.B.A. FM B.H.U.)

Ans:

Category	Value in %	Value of Material (₹)
A	59	2,11,800
B	27	95,600
C	14	50,820

14. A manufacturing company is using Material 'X' as its raw material for producing the product. The cost of material is ₹ 12 per kg and its input-output ratio 130%. On account of short supply of material 'X', the company wants to use substitute materials 'Y' and 'Z' without sacrificing the quality of the product. The following information are available for materials 'Y' and 'Z':

Material	Rate per kg	Input-output Ratio
Y	₹ 10	125%
Z	₹ 11	110%

You are required to recommend which material is to be used.

Ans: Cost per kg material Y ₹ 12.50 and Z ₹ 12.10. Decision: Material Z is preferred

15. Following information are obtained from the records of Kunal Ltd.:

	₹
Credit Sales	5,50,000
Cash Sales	1,00,000
Return Inward	50,000
Opening Inventory	50,000
Closing Inventory	70,000
Gross Profit Ratio on Cost 25%	

You are required to calculate:

(i) Cost of Goods Sold

(ii) Inventory Turnover Ratio

(iii) Inventory Conversion Period

Ans: (i) Cost of goods sold ₹ 4,80,000, (ii) Inventory Turnover Ratio 8 times and (iii) Inventory Conversion Period 46 days

16. Kalyani Manufacturers Ltd. manufactures mobile screen. The following details are available from the books of account regarding material consumption:

Maximum stock level	3,000 units
Minimum stock level	1,000 units
Re-ordering quantity	2,000 units
Material consumption	12,000 units

Find out:

(i) Material Turnover Ratio

(ii) Material Conversion Period

Ans: (i) 6 times, and (ii) 61 days

Index

ABC analysis, 132, 136
Absolute liquid ratio, 55
Accounting of inventories, 80
Accrual accounts, 47
Adequate working capital, 61
Aggressive approach, 51

Bank balance, 20
Bills discounting, 49
Bond, 44
Business cycle, 18

Capital cost, 72
Carrying costs, 128
Cash balance, 20
Cash credit, 48
Cash-to-cash conversion cycle, 9
Classification of inventory, 110
Codification, 110
  methods, 111
Commercial banks, 48
Commercial paper (CP), 47
Conservative approach, 49
Consumables, 72
Core current assets, 43
Cost accounting standard-6 (CAS-6), 83
Credit availability, 18
Credit policy, 17
Current assets, 5
Current liabilities, 5, 6
Current ratio, 43, 54

Debentures, 44
Debtors, 20
Discrepancies, 137
Diversification of business, 18

Economic factors, 19
Economic order quantity (EOQ), 128
Economic purchasing, 77
EOQ model, 129
Estimating working capital, 19
  techniques, 20
Excess working capital, 62

Factoring, 47
Financial management
  objective, 13
Financing of
  long-term working capital, 43
  short-term working capital, 43, 45
  working capital, 43
Finished goods, 71, 75, 76
First-in-First out (FIFO) method, 94, 98
Fixed capital, 13
FSN analysis, 144
Funds, 77

GOLF analysis, 145
Gross operating cycle, 10
Gross working capital, 5, 7
Gross working capital turnover ratio, 58

Hedging approach, 53
HML analysis, 145
Holding inventories, 73, 75

Inflated price method, 104
Input-output ratio, 141
Interval measure, 57
Inventories, 20, 70, 71

Inventory control, 77, 120, 122
financial objectives, 121
control ratios, 140
control techniques, 123
conversion period, 142
cost, 72
management, 69, 78
turnover ratio, 141
valuation, 79, 91
Issue management, 79

Just-in-time (JIT) system, 138, 139, 140

Last-in-First out (LIFO) method, 96, 98
Lead time, 112
Liberal credit policy, 17
credit terms, 18
Long-term loans, 44

Management attitude, 19
Manufacturing cycle, 16
Material loss, 83
management, 82

Nature of business, 15
Net operating cycle, 11
Net working capital, 5, 6, 7

Obsolescence index, 89
Obsolete items, 87, 88
Operating cycle, 9, 14
method, 20, 26
performance, 19
Ordering cost, 72, 128
Outstanding expenses, 21
Overdraft, 49
Overstocking, 77, 105, 106
costs, 73

Packing materials, 72
Percentage of sales, 20
method, 23
Permanent working capital, 7, 43
Perpetual inventory system, 136
Physical objectives, 120
Precautionary motive, 74
Price level changes, 17
Procurement of materials, 79
Production policy, 16
Public deposits, 44

Quantity, 128
Quick ratio, 54

Raw materials, 71, 74, 76
conversion period, 143
demand estimation, 78
turnover ratio, 143
Realisable price method, 105
Regression analysis, 20, 25
Regular working capital, 8
Replacement price method, 105
Replenishment policy, 113
Reserve working capital, 8
Retained earnings, 44
Return on investment, 52
Risk management, 80

Sales forecasting, 80
Scrap, 84
SDE analysis, 145
Seasonal factors, 16
variations, 16
working capital, 8
Share capital, 43
Short-term loans, 48
Simple average price method, 99
Size of business, 16
SOS analysis, 145
Special working capital, 8
Spoilage, 85
Standard price method, 102
Stock balance, 137
Stock levels, 124
Stock of finished goods, 20
raw materials, 20
Stockout costs, 73
Stock turnover or sales, 18
Storage costs, 73

Storage loss index, 89
Storage management, 79
Storekeeping, 110
Stores, 108, 109
Strict credit policy, 17
Sundry creditors, 21
Sundry materials, 72
Supply chain management, 80

Techniques of inventory control, 144
Temporary or variable working capital, 8, 43
Total operating cycle period, 26
Trade credit, 45, 46
Trade-off, 53
Transaction motive, 74
Types of inventories, 71

Understocking, 107

Variable capital, 13
VED analysis, 144

Warehouse management, 80
Wastage, 83
Weighted average price method, 101
Working capital, 4
    objectives, 14
    influencing factors, 15
Working capital cycle, 17
Working capital finance, 48
Working capital financing mix, 49
    strategies, 49
Working capital management, 4, 49
    symptoms of poor management, 63
Working capital ratio, 53
Working capital turnover ratio, 58
Work-in-progress, 10, 20, 71, 75